MADNESS AND ME

MY SEARCH FOR SANITY

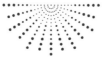

LISA SUZANNE NUGENT

Editing by Fred Johnson / Standout Books

Design and Layout by Standout Books

ISBN 978-1797580562

The Other Side of Madness

Mad, crazy, psycho, mental, nuts, manic and *schizoid* are all words or labels that have been used to describe my mother. But what is 'poor' mental health anyway, and who is to say what is bad or normal? There are naturally people out there who may appear a little odd and who act differently to the others around them, but who is crazy? Is it the woman who walks in a straight line down a street or is it the woman who skips in zigzags? Who's the odd one?

From the times of Hippocrates in the fifth century BC, humankind has been striving to heal the sick mind. Some cultures still believe mental illness is due to demonic possession or religious punishment, but from as early as the 1840s science has taken the lead in treating the mentally ill.

'It makes all sorts to make a world,' my mum used to say, and she is right. It would be a rather boring world if we were all the same, but is that boring world actually the safest place to be?

The 'unwell' stamp on my mum's forehead was fixed long ago. It sinks ever deeper with every maddening year, and all the medications and treatments she's received have either been ineffective or, worse, served only to uphold the mark. So why has the title 'mad' been assigned to my mum? I only assume that for some people, my mum's oddities and dark moments are hard to understand. The mad individual's internal beats and cycles tick at the same speed as anyone else's, but the mind gathers so much momentum that it spins off into overdrive. The thoughts of the mad catapult the mind into a different realm, from which the mind struggles to return, leaving the person confused and weak. Many never return, remaining instead in a world they learn to live in and be controlled by, for this is far easier than battling with their own demons.

For a few, madness takes on a different, dark meaning. There is a side to madness that is hidden and forgotten, a side that is uncontrolled and unpredictable, a side that is evil. My mum lives with this madness: a violent insanity that toys with its victims until they can no longer see the line between right and wrong. It controls their every thought, their every action, until it is the only voice they hear. The evil voice of my mother's madness ruled our lives without respite or compassion, leaving a family with wounds that never healed. We lived in silent torment, the voice in Mum's head deciding our every move, our every fear. It controlled and tormented us just as it did Mum, but it remained concealed, leaving us tap-dancing on the thin glass of madness, waiting for the hairline cracks to break.

* * *

So why did the voice of evil choose Mum as its vessel? Was she born with a genetic predisposition, or was her madness learnt? Did she allow it to take hold of a malrotated genome – a disease with no toxic chemicals to kill it – or was it instilled in her mind by an outside force? Were there parental influences conditioning the mind? Just as Pavlov trained his dogs to salivate at the ring of a bell, did Mum learn to listen to the voice that permeated her thoughts, allowing that voice to control her actions? If there is a history of tormented minds in a family, then does genetics win the argument?

Personally, I don't buy it; I don't believe that one faulty gene can send so much misery cascading down the genetic tree. I believe that the diversity of the human species and the influences of personal ideologies derail this theory, suggesting that genetics alone is not the culprit. Intelligent animals learn new behaviours and traits that facilitate evolution and adaptation to an environment that constantly changes around them. If we do not adapt, we do not survive. The human mind has a huge capacity and thirst for learning, resulting in the exponential pace of development, so if a child is born into an environment of cruelty and depression, is it not reasonable to suggest that the child will learn and develop the traits and behaviours of his or her teachers? If Mum was born into an environment that bred displacement and torment, would the madness and evil – which, to Mum, appeared the norm – spread to her? If so, what hope is there for my sister and me?

* * *

I am bound by the forces of the earth,
I am bound by the ticking of time,
I am bound by the muscles of my body and
I am bound by the commands of God.
I am bound by the laws that are written, and
I am bound by the order of nature, so
How do I rewrite the bounds of my memories?
How do I cut free the bounds of my mind?

* * *

I thought I might be dead. I was lying on the slightly dirty cream-coloured carpet, and my body wouldn't move. My brain was telling my lungs to expand and deflate, but no oxygen seemed to enter or leave. My breath was shallow and pathetic; my mouth was dry and sticky. How the fuck did I get here? Did I have a heart attack? Was I bleeding out from a major artery in my neck?

I was unsure if this was reality or a dream.

It was not a delusion – I felt the harsh bristles of the carpet fibres against my cheek, and I heard the dull hum of the boiler igniting as the temperature fell. I strained to move the muscles in my arms, but the blood did not seem to want to flow. The breath I had was not enough to form words.

'Are you going to move?' my husband said coldly.

I didn't blame him for the venom in his voice – I knew I deserved every twisted word he breathed, as it was my desire to leave. He had done nothing wrong – he never hit me, was never unfaithful – but though I could not justify my decision, I knew I had to go.

I thought of my dad, my marriage, the life I hoped I would have and the life I was forced to live. The feeling was totally consuming, and it absorbed the energy I needed to move the muscles in my mouth to reply to the man standing over me. He left the room without another word, leaving me in exile with cries stuck in my throat.

* * *

I carried a little of his broken heart with me that day in the knowledge that this situation was all down to me. I was a selfish, wicked person, and I hated everything about myself, even down to the lashes that batted away the torrent of tears flowing effortlessly down my cheeks. I felt the weight of Dad's death on my shoulders. The experiences of my past had done nothing to prepare me for the tests of life, and I'd failed to change what nature or genetics or God had preordained. I'd felt this low only three times in my life, and I can honestly say that I had never been as close to the bottom as I was that day. I felt unworthy of this life and wanted to be punished for the thoughts that I had. I thought that the world, my family and my daughter would flourish without me, unburdened by a mum, wife and human being who had nothing to contribute.

It would have been easy to stay upon the cream carpet and let death take me like debris after a storm. I felt that death was my friend, promising to eliminate all that was wrong with me in one easy motion. My body was heavy, and I felt my life sinking through the carpet and into the wooden slats below. My blood and skin mingled with the timbers that held the walls in place.

'Mummy, Mummy, I am hungry.'

That's all it took. As adrenaline surged through my lifeless veins, the glue began to dissolve. Oxygen returned to my muscles, allowing them to contract, and my limbs extended. My breath returned, allowing me to smile into the angelic face of my daughter.

Hayley saved my life that day. She made me realise that this life is not about me, you or the postman; it's about the evolutionary circle. Whatever happens to you or me, the world will continue. As long as you return your organic body to the earth, the ether doesn't care if you're happy or sad, contented or misled. Life wasn't going to get up and make Hayley dinner; it had to be me. If you have an ounce of consciousness, you grit those pearly whites and you suck it up, for what you receive in return may be truly beautiful.

That was then, and this is now.

1

BREATHING UNDERWATER

You are who you are, nothing more, nothing less.
Nothing can truly change this but you.
Love the good bits, move past the bad.
No regrets, no hate, no blame.
Be mindful, be awake, be alive, for it is precious,
THIS LIFE.

As I wake up in the swimming pool that is my bed, I take
two life-giving breaths and peel my knickers off my sticky
bottom. I am trying to decide whether it would be better to
tuck the belly below the waistband of my jeans or to just let
it roam free. I am hoping that no one notices the neon-
white flesh peeking out below my jumper, telling everyone
that I've lost control of my body. What the hell are hot
flushes, anyway? What purpose do they have? Are they just
another of Mother Nature's cruel jibes? Is she up there
laughing her pretty, line-free face off? I wonder if she's

eating chocolate, drinking beer and pushing her supple, lard-free, perfectly rounded bottom in my sweaty red face.

Why is it that on those rare occasions when you feel good about the few attributes you have left, Mother Nature manages to move your makeup from your eyes to your cheeks and causes that lovingly coiffured fringe to stick to your forehead, making you look like a mad woman from a horror film? Or, better, a comedy spoof – and you are the leading lady stumbling from one cringe-inducing moment to the next.

One day my superintendent at work will discover that I have no idea how I became an advanced practitioner radiographer who spends the day sticking tubes and catheters into almost every orifice of the human body. I think that maybe I have escaped discovery, that maybe I can continue pretending to be an experienced radiographer who knows exactly what she is doing. In fact, this persona hides a fumbling optimist who spends her time trying to make people smile even when they're having a rectal tube inserted.

I am, after many years of doubt, an eternally positive person, but I wasn't born this way; rather, it took many years to make the conscious decision to change. After a very long time spent being negative and self-critical, believing that the world was resisting my quest for happiness at every opportunity, I stopped. I stopped looking at the empty space in front of me and started to fill it with memories that would make me smile. I started to look at people and situations from a different angle, a different dimension if you like. I started to wear their shoes, remembering what I was feeling when I screamed and swore at Mum or when I blankly ignored people, unable to find the words to reply to their simple question.

Once, when waiting to pay for petrol at my local station, the young disinterested girl at the till asked me the number of the pump where my car sat. I looked at her as if she had asked me the meaning of life in Mandarin; I just couldn't process her simple question. She repeated the question in a louder, slower voice, wondering if I was deaf or just stupid. Again I stared at her, this time thinking she was speaking Russian. I looked behind myself, hoping to find an answer somewhere in the carpark, but realised as I stared at my car that I didn't know what I was supposed to be looking for. 'Is it the silver car?' she shouted, in my native English this time.

'Yes,' I replied, wondering why she wanted to know the colour of my car. So, was I entering the throes of a breakdown? Was I having a stroke, or was I simply in China? Most likely, my mind had tripped the off switch and defaulted to emergency lighting, leaving me standing alone in a dimly lit corridor. There was just enough light to guide me back to the car after handing over my card to the now-stroppy teenager tutting loudly under her breath. Free from the foreign world of the petrol station, I pulled into a lay-by and cradled my head in my sweaty hands. What was wrong with me? Does the mind have a safe-mode function that automatically stops you from downloading the hidden virus threatening to corrupt your precious files?

So why am I not sitting in a high-winged tartan chair,

dribbling down my nylon nightie, in a home with safety locks on the windows and buzzers at every door? Has the genetic tree finally wrapped its branches around me? Thankfully, the stable arms of Dad and the companionship of my twin sister helped preserve the glass foundation we danced on, the faint spider lines holding out even through thunderstorms and earthquakes. We held hands, knowing we had each other to hold on to as the spider lines crackled and danced.

Why have I chosen to immortalise my life story now? Why at all? I'm not really sure. Is it a cathartic exercise or an attempt to prove that I am more than just a wife, mother and radiographer? A philosopher would say that if we do not pick apart and examine our lives, then those lives are not worth living; it would be like continuing a routine without stopping to check whether what we are doing is right for us and the world around us. But what if, after picking apart said life, we found it was not worth examining in the first place? The philosopher would ask, *would you board an aeroplane that had not been examined for broken wings or a working engine? And if the wings had been found to be broken, would you not want them to be fixed?* Maybe if we all took a moment to reflect and examine our wings, we would become better people, and maybe being better people would provide us with the rare clarity of thought that brings happiness a little closer.

* * *

After pondering all this for a full and lengthy forty-seven years, it finally comes to me. I am writing this book to ask permission. Throughout my life, I have longed for and desperately needed approval from others – but how could I expect approval from others when I couldn't even approve of myself? I think that's why it has taken so long to write this book. I just couldn't believe that I was good enough to do it. Even now, I am consumed by feelings of inadequacies and doubt, which have often condemned this manuscript to the back of the drawer for months on end.

As a fully grown and reasonably intelligent woman, I still try to justify every past and present thought and emotion I have ever had. *Should I feel this way? Should I have had that thought? Is this normal? Am I bad?* When the terrifying moments come and I actually have to express how I might be feeling or ask for what I so desperately need, the anxiety starts to bubble. The pounding starts first. It builds and builds until the pulsating of my heart beats so violently against my sternum that it takes my breath away. Then the sweat starts to gather until it begins to trickle from my brow. I shuffle uncomfortably as my clothes start to stick to me, and my breath becomes shallow until I find that I can't form the words anymore. The prickling sensation starts at the back of my throat and proceeds to sweep quickly and without mercy along my arms and abdomen until an itchy, burning rash covers me. The words are trapped in my heart, bound by fear and uncertainty. I can't let them free because it doesn't matter what I think and it doesn't matter what I want – whatever I have to say is going to be wrong. I struggle with the words I should be screaming out loud and decide it's easier to keep them there until my heart is so full of words that there's no room left for me anymore.

I need permission to let some of these words out. I want to say them out loud without prejudice or judgment from others, to say them without fear of anxiety or reprisal. I so desperately want someone to say, 'You're not an evil person, Lisa. You're just normal.' I am striving for the day when I have the ability to speak or express my wishes without having to take a deep breath and gather my nerve. If I could actually put things straight in my head, I could actually shout these words out: *Is it okay to have feelings of hate for and disconnection from your own mother? Is it okay to dwell on poor old me?* Shell and I still find it impossible to speak of certain events, but we can now have conversations without mental breakdowns or angry explosions. If we don't approach our past now, the past may approach us, and I am sure its course will not be kind or forgiving.

Shell looks at me through the screen of my tablet and grins. She's wrapped in a heavy jumper and hugs her knees. 'It's bloody minus thirty-five today.'

'That's what you get for marrying a Canadian,' I say while rubbing my arms against the imaginary cold. She laughs and calls me a wimp.

'I was in bed this morning, playing with my boobs, and I thought I might start writing a book about us,' Shell says without acknowledging the strange and slightly weird statement.

'I can't believe you just said that!' I say, laughing.

'About the boobs or the book?'

'Both! What have boobs got to do with writing a book?'

Shell takes a breath in and contemplates her answer. 'It made me think of when I used to climb into your bed every night.'

A subdued snort leaves my nose as I remember.

'And your snoring!' Shell says through a huff of laughter.

'Hey, don't be cheeky to your older sister.'

'Older by one whole minute,' Shell retorts. 'Do you remember what we used to say?'

In unison we recite the ritual: 'Do you have enough room? Do you have enough blanket? Are you warm enough?' We roar with laughter at the childish memories. Shell's laughter fades, mirroring my own feelings. 'Why did you always end up in my bed, anyway?' I ask, pulling myself from the visions in my mind.

'Because it was the hardest bedroom for Mum to get into.' A sad smile forms as I remember the sliding door Dad fitted to give my boxy room a bigger feel. It would get stuck on the rails and was so heavy it needed a double-handed push to open. Shell shifts in her seat and then the screen freezes. I wait for it to reconnect, but all I see are the corners of her mouth drawn down with heaviness and eyes full of sadness looking back at me. The screen flickers back into action, and my attention is brought back into the present.

'You're back!' I say, stating the obvious. 'So, tell me about this book idea.'

Shell looks up as if looking for the answer written on

the ceiling. 'I had a difficult phone call from Mum yesterday. I was not happy when she phoned at five a.m., by the way.'

'You know Mum has no concept of time.'

Shell pauses and looks at her feet. 'It just brought all those awful feelings back.'

Dread fills my chest. 'What did she say?'

'The usual. "I hate you," "I want to die" and a lot of screaming. You know the routine.'

I sigh deeply. 'We've had a couple weeks of peace, so we were due a breakdown.'

Shell lets out a small huff of air. 'I wondered if writing it all down would help?'

'In a book, you mean?'

'Yeah. What do you think?'

'I am no good at writing; you know how bad I am at spelling!'

'Oh, blimey yeah. Even spell check can't figure out your spelling!' Shell replies mockingly.

'Okay, it's not that funny,' I say in playful defence.

'Why don't we write a chapter each and see how it goes?' Shell says with excitement in her voice.

'Okay, why not.'

A week passes before I finished my chapter. With all its spelling mistakes and rawness, I read it to Shell.

I sink down into my bed and cover my head with my blanket. My eight-year-old twin sister Shell, hides her face between the fold of my night dress. We hold our breath – listening. If we don't move, she won't find us. A scream vibrates up the stairs. Shell clings to me tighter and sobs.

'You're trying to kill me!' The voice screams. We sink deeper into the bed.

'Be quiet,' I whisper to Shell.

'But I am scared'. We freeze as we hear the familiar thud on the stairs. One haunting step at a time. I listen to the heavy, angry breath and I could feel the venom on its tongue. It screams again 'Why are you trying to kill me?'. We start to panic, and we fail to hold onto the sobs. Its outside our door now and I hear the hands trying to slide it open. My own hot breath suffocates me under the blankets and I can't breathe, but still we don't move.

The door slides open. Shell grips my arm so tight it hurts. I feel something hover above me.

'You hate me, you are evil.' The voice can see us now. Not caring that we can be heard we both begin to cry. I don't understand, I don't hate her, I don't want her to die. I feel the static crackle in the air as the voice remains. I can't stop the noise of my cries. I bury my face into Shells shoulder and recite in my head repeatedly. 'Please god, make it go away'.

Shell sits quietly and doesn't respond.

'Is it that bad?'

She takes a breath in and rubs her fingers into her damp eyes. 'No, it's not bad, it's just hard to hear it.' We both sit silent, trying to resist the tears. Shell takes a loud breath in before saying, 'I don't think I can do it. You write it for the both of us.'

* * *

So, like many other souls of this world, Shelley and I have spent our lives bobbing up and down with our sweetly smiling faces above water while our legs kick and thrash below. This is manageable for a while – the smiles remain believable, and the kicking stays strong – but eventually the legs get tired and the cheeks start to sag.

In that huge expanse of cold, dark water, you cannot see past your knees, and all around you unseen creatures swim a hair's breadth from your feet. Some may glide majestically between the turmoil of your legs or play hide-and-seek with the panicked thrashing of your hands, but they mean you no harm, while others snake silently from the depths with cruelty in their eyes. It is these creatures that we fear.

The beasts that hunt us are large and predatory. They can smell a single drop of blood from many miles away, allowing them to track the weak and wounded. Their sharp sense of hearing targets the panicked thrashing of the drowning victim, and they hone in on the sound. As Shell and I bob up and down with the silent creatures of the sea, we hold each other's hands and kick hard. Occasionally a shadow will pass beneath our feet, just out of reach. When the hunter makes its move, at first it toys with us, passing just inches from our feet, testing the strength and reactions of its prey. It waits, circling, allowing its prey to become weaker and weaker, until it feels the fight leave the panicked kicks. When the smell of fear becomes intoxicating and overpowering, its primal urges force it to strike.

* * *

I've been told that to dream about breathing underwater represents mastery of your own emotions or coping with challenging episodes in your life. I haven't ever had that dream. I have had plenty of the common anxiety dreams – for example, the one where you're naked and running, exposed, to the laughing world. Your legs are so heavy that they won't move, so you remain standing in the crowded street, unable to lift your feet, your whole body straining forwards without movement. You can now feel the eyes of the onlookers burning as they observe boobs swaying and belly wobbling, and there is nothing but cold, clammy hands to hide your vulnerability. Or perhaps I am hanging off a cliff by my fingertips – it's usually a cliff hundreds of feet above a beach, and beyond, the waves crash upon the shore in anger. The sky is black with storm clouds. The dream never seems to have an ending, either happy or sad, instead leaving me there hanging and naked. I often wake in a cold sweat, frantically feeling for my knickers, my fingertips still curled against the edge of the cliff.

While breathing underwater in our dreams may supposedly represent mastery over our emotions, why that particular image? What is the brain trying to tell us? It is inconceivable to think that, as humans, we could learn how to breathe without oxygen. For some, breathing underwater and the emotional mastery that comes with it are learnt behaviours: skills that develop from the need to survive. When you have seen the rocks at the bottom of the ocean, you eventually learn how to float above them. Actual *breathing* is a little harder to master, but the alternative is to sink, to feel your lungs fill up with water . . . and that is the easiest moment to give in, to let the ocean win and the hunters take you. To breathe, to float above the hunters – this is the hardest part. To me, the paddlers are the strongest people, the truly brave. To resist the easy arms of the dark water is a battle to be fought every day, and to win is a truly courageous act.

* * *

You may ask, how does one learn to breathe underwater, to resist the hunters? What are the secrets to a happy life? Do we find the answers in science, or does God hold the key? Can we find joy in possessions or in being loved and loving someone in return? I feel that happiness is a very personal destination that differs from one person to the next. For me, happiness is one word: appreciation. You may ask how you can be appreciative and thankful after all that life has handed you. Indeed, on occasion I have echoed that very question – but it is because I have experienced those painful times that I now appreciate the good. Poet Percy Bysshe Shelley asks, 'If winter comes, can spring be far behind?' Perhaps not, but for some, winter rages long and bitter, and the falling flakes of snow never seem to cease. During my own unending winters, I would stop and examine the white crystals and try to see the magic that they brought. I would appreciate their beauty and the miracle of their presence. On occasion, I would wake without the ability to appreciate the snow or the sun that warmed my face or the soft carpet that massaged my feet; I would instead frame all that was good as a personal attack. Some days, fairness became an ideology, an enigma that eluded me. I questioned the very softness of the carpet beneath my feet, instead perceiving coarseness.

For me, it isn't a question of why all these bad things have happened to me; it's a question of how I will cope with those things. Only by answering this question can I start to appreciate the warmth that the carpet affords me and how the sun has, at this exact moment, entered through the exact window pane that directs its healing arms around my pale, cold face.

2

FLOATING IN A BUBBLE, HOLDING HANDS: THE STORY BEGINS

Jean opened the front door to silence. 'Come on, Linda,' she said as she took the hand of her younger sister and guided her into the hallway. 'Mum, we're home.' The two young girls stood at the threshold of the kitchen to find the woman peeling potatoes. She didn't seem to hear at first but remained focused on the movement of the blade. 'Mum,' Jean repeated as she stood at the doorway, still holding Linda's hand.

'For God's sake, Jean, do you always have to sneak up on me like that?' Gladys said as she slammed the potato peeler onto the kitchen worktop.

'But Mum . . .'

Gladys took a slow, deep breath and continued to peel the potato in her hand. Still Jean didn't move but only saw the white bandages wrapped tightly around each of her mum's wrists.

'Mum?' Jean said with anxiety rising in her voice. 'What's wrong with your wrists?'

Her mother stopped and slowly placed the peeled potato back on the work surface. She hesitated before turning to face her two daughters.

She stooped in front of her twelve-year-old child. 'You must promise me, Jean, never to tell anyone about this. Especially your father.' As her fingers began to grip tighter around Jean's shoulders she whispered, 'Promise me?' Jean stood rigid and silent, still mesmerised by the blood seeping through the wrappings of her wrists. 'Jean!' Gladys started to shake Jean in the throes of panic. 'Promise me?'

The sound of a key turning in the front door shook Gladys from the tense moment. Her eyes widened, and the colour drained from her face. Jean could see the panic rise in the dullness of her blue eyes looking back at her. 'Take Linda up to your room and don't come down until I tell you.' Gladys didn't wait for a reply, but instead she ushered the girls towards the stairs.

'Bill, you're back early from work today.' All three stopped suddenly by the bottom step. Gladys stood with her arms behind her back and silently used her fingers to pull the sleeves of her top down to cover the evidence of her unhappiness.

Gladys's eyes never left those of the man that stood before them. 'Upstairs, girls. I'll call you when dinner's ready.' Jean swiftly manoeuvred past her mother and urged her sister to follow. The six-year-old Linda didn't move but instead remained glued to the spot. She looked directly at the man without smiling, her eyes narrow and mouth taut. 'Linda, upstairs now!' her mother shouted with authority. Linda moved with defiance in her step, her eyes never leaving those of the watchful man.

'Why do you do that?' Jean asked as Linda jumped onto her bed. 'You know that it makes Daddy mad.'

'I don't like Daddy sometimes,' she replied, burying her head in the soft flannelette case of the pillow.

'He works hard, and it makes him grumpy. Just ignore it.' Linda didn't reply but continued to hide her face. The rumbling of an argument vibrated through the walls of the house, and both girls stiffened with anxiety and anticipation. Linda sat up and crawled across the bed so that she sat close to her sister, her eyes reddened and skin pale. Their silent communication was broken by the cries of a baby. 'Look what you have done now! It's your fault that they are arguing, and now they've woken David up.'

'It's not my fault,' Linda shouted as Jean left the room to comfort the youngest of the family.

The dinner table was laid with a pristine white cloth with the fold lines still evident. Gladys and the children sat with plates of chicken and potatoes before them, while Bill sat in his large brown armchair with a beer in his hand. The only sound to break the silence was the ticking of the grandfather clock, which stood with authority by the living-room door.

'Linda, eat your peas,' Gladys said with a glare.

'I don't like them,' Linda retorted and leaned back in her chair with folded arms.

'Do as your mother tells you,' Bill said as he joined the table and sat next to Gladys, his eyes still fixed on his youngest daughter. Linda didn't move. Bill paused and then calmly began to slice the meat off the chicken leg on his plate. Linda remained still. Her once-pursed lips relaxed, and her eyes lost the hardness of her original disobedience. Jean shuffled in her chair and stopped eating as David began to cry. Bill replaced his knife and fork on his plate and looked directly into the eyes of his daughter. 'If you aren't going to eat your peas, then you won't have any dinner. Now go to your room, and I will come see you later.'

Linda sat bolt upright, and she quickly moved her panicked gaze onto her mother. 'Don't look at me, young lady, you brought this on yourself.'

Linda stood, but before leaving the table she paused. 'Mum, please, I don't want to go to my room on my own.'

'Don't be silly. Now do as your father said.' Linda slowly stood and left, her face now a picture of regret and sadness. Before hiding under the blankets of her bed, she pulled a chair in front of her door and placed her stuffed rabbit on the seat. 'Good night, bunny. Keep me safe tonight.'

The next morning the house felt cold and dark, reflecting the mood of the family. Gladys sat silently at the table, with her hand gently stroking the bruise that had developed over her right eye. Jean sat next to her and leaned her head on her mother's shoulder, but Gladys shrugged her off and tutted loudly. 'Go and get your brother and sister ready for school,' she said coldly.

'But what about breakfast?' Jean said, wiping tears from her eyes.

'There's no breakfast today. Now go away.'

After school Jean found Linda sitting in the garden with her back towards the sun. As Jean neared, she saw that Linda had a pair of scissors in her hand. Looking over Linda's shoulder, Jean took a sharp breath in and stumbled back. At Linda's feet lay what looked like small maggots.

'What are you doing?' Jean stammered.

'I like to see them wriggle when I cut them up.' Linda picked up a portion of worm and waved it in front of Jean.

'That's so cruel. I am going to tell Mum.'

Linda immediately jumped to her feet and screamed at her sister. 'Don't you dare! I will tell them that you broke the vase in the living room, and you'll be in real trouble.' Jean stepped back and swallowed down the lump that was forming in her throat.

'What's all this noise?' The angry voice of Bill boomed down the garden, and both girls froze.

The tall, striking figure of their father strode down the path, his face taut with eyes wild.

'Jean's cutting up worms,' Linda shouted as she flicked her narrow eyes at Jean.

'That's not true!' Jean said as she stepped back from her father, shaking her head.

Bill stood with his hands on his hips and turned to Linda. 'Don't lie to me, young lady.'

'But it . . .'

Bill took a step nearer, and as his hand left his hip Linda turned and ran.

'He's hitting me!' she shouted as she ran into the street. 'My dad's hitting me.'

'Linda, get back here,' Bill screamed, running after her. Linda spun on her heels to face her father and calmly said, 'No.' As Bill raised his hand again he was suddenly aware of his neighbour standing at her door, witnessing the commotion. 'Linda, get inside now,' he spat through gritted teeth.

Linda smirked and remained still. Bill relaxed his rigid stance and placed his hands in his pockets. He grinned at Linda and snorted. 'I'll give you sixpence if you come inside.'

Linda remained motionless as she considered his offer. Her gaze never left him as she walked past and went inside.

* * *

In September 1970, the five-foot-one, eight-stone Linda from Dagenham, Essex gave birth to rather large twin girls. Shelley Jane (or Shell as we came to call her) was a respectable six-pounds-nine, and Lisa Suzanne, who narrowly escaped being called Ursula (I think Mum had just been watching that James Bond film where Ursula Andress walks out of the sea in that bikini), was a heftier seven-pounds-one. As you can imagine, this was quite traumatic for Linda, who had a petite frame, so Shell and I were brought into this world via a hole cut into her abdomen. It wasn't just Mum's small stature that was to blame; Shell decided to make a statement by trying to look backwards while leaving the safety of our bubble. Perhaps she had already decided she didn't like the look of this world.

In the corridors of East Ham's general hospital paced the man who was going to try his best to hold it all together. Terry was a six-foot-two ex-bodybuilder from the depths of the East End. His towering frame and strong, sturdy, but quiet demeanour painted him as a man of control. Terry was a true East End geezer with whom not even the biggest of men would choose to pick a fight. Beneath the tower of muscle he hid a soul made of love and kindness; he was the sort of man who would return home with a potted flower for each of his girls to place by her bed. He was a man who would melt at his daughters' hugs and surrender his last pennies so that they could buy toffee on a Saturday night. Terry was a quiet man with a natural, comic wit. He didn't look like the typical comedian, so it surprised people when he did or said the unexpected, which in turn made him even funnier.

Our parents met in a genuine East End pub in Manor Park, London when Mum was just nineteen (Dad was a respectable two years her senior). Back then, Mum was a catch: petite and slender with long, dark, silky hair that reached below her shoulders. Her miniskirt emphasised her toned legs and slim waist, daring anyone not to full in love with her. So you can understand why Dad fell so quickly for the intelligent, quick-witted woman who would, two years later, become his wife and, a year after that, the mother to his twin daughters. It was easy to see why Mum fell for the strong man that could lift the petite Linda from the floor with one arm and fit her perfectly under his armpit, hiding her away from the world. From the very beginning, Dad was the answer; he represented an escape route from the demons that constantly followed her. He was the promise of deliverance and, perhaps, liberation.

There is a favourite photo of mine; it's the only photo of Mum and Dad that makes me feel happy. It must have been taken around 1968, just before they got married. Mum stands close to Dad, and they are holding hands. She's craning her neck upwards to look at him, her smile is genuine and her eyes glitter. It doesn't seem to matter to her that Dad isn't looking at her in the same way (instead, he grins awkwardly at the camera, squinting in the sun). They stand on the pavement outside my grandparents' house, a typical two-up-two-down terraced house on a nondescript street in Newham, London. Mum wears a miniskirt, and Dad wears a polo-neck jumper and jacket typical of the 1960s. I think this particular photo sticks in my mind because it truly makes my heart ache. To me, it proves that they did love one another. It gives a glimpse of what could have been: a normal life with the usual ups and downs. It's a time before it all, a time before we all knew, a time before it all ended.

The mind has a talent for memory. It has, as I imagine, rows and rows of boxes with closed lids, each containing one memory or image hidden away from the active part of the brain. Some of these boxes are easier to lift from the shelf than others, and at the back, dusty neglected ones teeter on the edge, inches away from being lost. Some boxes are made of stone. They stand firm, never in danger of falling off and being lost. They are hidden deep within the tunnels of shelves, in secret places that are not easily found; they are not easily opened, but they are never forgotten. They contain great and terrible things, things capable of evoking the greatest happiness and despair.

Something as simple as a smell or a sound can set off a journey along the tall stack of shelves. Having found the correct box, the mind unhinges the lid, letting the memory scuttle away towards the brain. The brain won't always use the memory in the most practical of ways – indeed, sometimes it'll have no idea what to do. For example, the sight of small, shiny mushrooms makes me want to run for the toilet as it brings back the memory and feeling of morning sickness. The deep, soothing tones of Elvis Presley bring memories of dancing. When Mum was happy, Shell and I would swing smoothly around her, dipping under her arms and spinning around to the rhythm of 'Jailhouse Rock' or 'Return to Sender,' trying to jive, while Dad swayed awkwardly like a demented chicken after too many espressos. Unfortunately for me, other happy memories have teetered off the shelf, and I wonder why I cannot recall them. Do the happy memories fade, or have I reinforced the bad ones by trying so hard to forget them? By continually replaying the bad times, have I cemented those dark boxes in place? To remember a happy time, one may take a photo or buy a memento that acts as a constant reminder of the happiness that was felt.

My memento is Mum, but she carries the bad as well as the good.

Other memories would bring happiness that would suddenly end in a sickening thud. One such memory was of Shell and I sat in the back seat of Dad's car. The excitement of a family camping trip made us giggle to the old dad jokes that had been cracked many times before: 'If you want to make the car go faster, you have to bounce up and down on the seat.' Shell and I responded to Dad's command, and the car accelerated as we hysterically threw ourselves around in our seats. Dad laughed as he watched in the rear-view mirror while Mum remained silent, only seeing the road ahead. After hours on the road we arrived at the busy camp-site in Cornwall, and Dad erected the orange-and-brown tent while Shell and I excitedly played tag. Mum sat in her silent world, smoking yet another cigarette without leaving the safety of the car. We ate fish and chips from the site café and drank tea made on a borrowed gas burner. As darkness fell Mum was oddly quiet and unwilling to join her family. She sat, quiet but observant, unwilling to leave her cocoon.

'Okay girls, time for spooky stories in bed.' Dad formed his hands into claws and growled. Shell and I rolled our eyes but quickly snuggled into our sleeping bags in excited anticipation. 'Lynn, are you coming?'

'No,' she spat. 'Go make happy families without me.' She turned away and returned to her seat in the car, still clutching the plastic cup of cold tea. It wasn't long before the real monster arrived. We woke in the night to the sound of the monster pacing the perimeter of the tent. It was subtle at first, just heavy breathing and the occasional rustle of nylon fabric as it brushed against the sides of the tent. Then the voice came. 'I want to go!' it demanded. 'Take me fucking home, you bastards!' We closed our eyes and covered our ears with our hands, only hearing our rapid breathing between the silent pauses. She screamed, and my heart began to thump hard with embarrassment. I stole a look toward Dad's sleeping bag, and I could see the whites of his eyes penetrating the darkness. His body lay perfectly still, seemingly without breathing, until Mum's tea cup came flying through the unzipped door of the tent, narrowly missing my feet. 'Right, that's it!' he said as he jumped onto his feet. 'In the car, girls.'

We obeyed without question and hurriedly gathered our things in our arms. Mum sat in the passenger seat, and without speaking she waited as Dad tore down the tent and bundled everything in the car boot in a knot of tent poles and clothing. It was midnight, and we ran away from the campsite like criminals escaping the crime scene. This childhood memento only serves as a reminder of anxious and fearful family holidays. Fortunately family holidays came to an end.

On the other side, my memento of an old and slightly rusty white van provokes memories of happiness and safety. It's a happy but tainted reminder of a six-foot carpenter driving home on a Friday night to his three-bedroom council house on an estate in North Essex. His pockets were full of wood shavings that would cover the carpet when he finally climbed out of his work clothes, and the holes in his socks would reveal hot, smelly feet. These sights would act as a signal that we could relax: Dad was home. When Dad was home, the house became a safe zone. The atmosphere warmed and the underlying current stopped crackling, allowing Shell and me to surface from our safehouse under the stairs. From there, the pretence of a normal family life could begin.

* * *

Each day would bring a different scenario, and none of us would know which theme Mum had chosen until it blossomed in front of us. We'd silently celebrate if she was having a good day – I remember one Friday night, we all climbed into Dad's van and drove to the pub up the road. We would never go in, but would instead sit in the van in the carpark with lemonade and packets of cheese and onion crisps. Dad would have a pint and Mum a snowball. To this day, I still don't know why we never went inside. It may have been that Shell and I were too young to enter, but more likely, I think it was the uncertainty stopping us. There were very few occasions where, as a family, we could happily be in an unfamiliar social environment. The alien sense of strangers nearby would unnerve Mum, forcing her paranoia into overdrive. The shift could be swift and unpredictable, fluctuating from euphoria to irrational condemnation of others. On one occasion, the postman would be the most wonderful, kind and understanding person, while on another day, he would be a thief, stealing one shoe of every pair.

On a similar, indistinguishable night, Dad found Shell and me under the stairs, amongst the cobwebs and broken Hoovers. He found Mum sitting at the kitchen table, rocking fiercely back and forth, a cigarette about to burn the tips of her fingers and a small pile of ash lying unnoticed in her lap. She was talking to the ghost again. 'You fucking bastard,' she said. 'You fucking bastard.' Tears reddened her eyes. 'You're all fucking bastards. What have you done to me? Why do you want me dead?'

Dad sat with her, trying to placate the storm that was about to break. The answers he gave to her furious questions were not enough to quell her irritation, and as the inquest continued, Mum began to toy with the knife in her hand, gently stabbing the small point into the surface of the table. The red marks on her wrists seemed to glow in the dim kitchen. She moved quickly and skilfully, but the knife didn't head to her wrist, its usual destination – instead, it ripped through the air in an arc towards Dad's chest. Dad instinctively lifted his arms, and the blade pierced through his hand, leaving a small but deep wound that spurted blood across the table.

'What do you think you are doing, Lynn?' he said as he ran his hand under the flowing tap and then wrapped a tea towel around the wound. 'For God's sake, you can't keep doing this. I love you, Lynn, but please tell me how I can help you.' Mum sat silently, cradling her face in her hands. Loud, desperate sobs fill the air. 'What is it, Lynn? Please tell me.' With a quiver in his voice Dad knelt before her and took her hands from her face, his eyes now filling with tears. Still no words, no explanation was given, but instead she continued to rock back and forth. Dad leaned forwards, placing his head in her outstretched hands. His whispered words pled with her. 'Please get better, Lynn, please.'

* * *

As far as I am aware, Dad never once raised his hand to Mum, not even in defence or backlash. Even now, I can scarcely believe his restraint; it would have been so easy to submit to the urge to retaliate, to let the adrenaline take control of his actions. I cannot say whether he ever came close to hitting her back. Instead, Dad would be found wandering the streets at night, the cold, hard air and his fast pace apparently enough to extinguish his anger.

Trying to hide the violence from us was a losing battle for Dad; in our small house, the physical and verbal abuse swiftly became the backdrop to our lives. Dad died with many scars. Most were visible to the eye as raised, skin-coloured mounds, but it was the wounds hidden inside his head that cut the deepest. Unbeknownst to Dad, Shell and I felt every painful word and every wound that was inflicted upon his body. We buried these feelings deep, unable to save dad from the woman he loved.

3

THE RUNAWAY CHURCH

Do you ever find yourself walking down a street, looking at your feet and not caring whether you fall or walk into someone? Your feet are moving independently, carrying you forwards along a path that you are barely conscious of. It's a surprisingly comforting feeling, like being underwater. You're not breathing; you're floating. Your body is bound by the water, protected from the things around you. You don't feel the wind or hear the noises of life, and the outside cannot touch you or your thoughts; it's just you and the water. It's warm and it envelops you, supporting you, but you can choose when to leave, when to return to the path, where your feet slowly lead you back home.

Along that path, I would sometimes steal a look through someone's window and imagine the families inside. The mum would be cooking a roast chicken; the dad drinking beer and watching TV, shouting at Johnny because he'd be arguing with Susie over the last Bourbon biscuit. They'd go to Tesco on Saturday mornings, where Johnny might get a Pokémon toy if he was good and Susie a girls' magazine with the latest boy band on the front. On Sundays, if it was sunny, they'd go to the beach and eat homemade ham sandwiches and then, as a treat, ice cream cones with Flakes. That's what every family does, isn't it? Isn't that real life?

When I think back, I realise we did those things too. I remember normal things and even some happy times. We were a normal family that did normal family things – or, at least, we did what Shell and I *thought* was normal. Didn't every child cook their own dinner because their mum was asleep, knocked out by tranquillizers? Didn't every child steal away in the middle of the night to sleep in Dad's van when their mother rampaged around the living room, writing messages on the walls and topping cups of coffee with light bulbs, just like any other mum would?

When our school friends went on family picnics, they too would put saucepans on their heads if it rained, wouldn't they? If we went to the beach, Mum would skip down the promenade singing, 'Oh I do like to be beside the seaside,' just like any other mum, and when visitors came to the door we would hide behind the sofa as Mum laughed hysterically-just like any other Mum.

In the last year of primary school in 1980, Shelley and I both received awards. Shelley's was for academia and mine was for sport. It was unusual for twins to both win awards at the same time, and I remember standing on the stage with my certificate in my hand, smiling so hard that my face hurt. Shelley stood beside me with shaking, damp hands.

I didn't feel sad that neither Mum nor Dad was there. I think we would have been more shocked if they were, as Dad continually worked and Mum hated social events and would rather sleep. While standing there trying to relax my face, I heard my form tutor say to her colleague, 'It's such a shame that the twins' parents couldn't be here, but I hear their mum isn't well. I did phone her to tell her that it's a special occasion, but she was a bit strange, if you know what I mean.'

It happened on an ordinary day in 1980. There was no blustery rain or blistering, hot sun to describe, nor did the day take on any distinctive meaning. It was a customary school day like any other. As always, we walked home from school, the back-door key swinging around my neck on a length of wool. However, today we didn't need to use the key – the window to the back door was shattered, its glass on the ground at our feet. Two panicked men stood outside the open door with sorry, shaken expressions. At that moment, a shower of plastic medicine bottles rained down on us as Mum screamed. A high-pitched, desperate scream: 'Help me, help me!' The two men – helpless priests from the local church – looked upon us with pity. 'Go,' they said, 'go to the church. You will be safe there until your father gets home.'

Shelley and I sat on the steps of the church, too nervous to enter. We were silent, trying to make sense of what we had heard. It wasn't that we were dismayed by the performance we'd seen – this was just what happened sometimes. Don't all Mums get sad and scared and cry a lot? So why did the men tell us to leave? We would just take the knife from Mum's hands and put her to bed, as we always did.

We never saw the priests again. Just like the countless health professionals and specialist doctors who'd abandoned us, they left us to pick up the broken glass and continue our lives in the background.

Shell and I both knew it was going to be a bad night, but it was even worse than we imagined. The tension in the house was unbearable. The anger crackled, and the eggshells didn't even hurt underfoot anymore. We huddled together, wondering not if, but when it would all begin. When would the heavy footsteps fall on the stairs? When would the heavy breathing start? When would the screaming pierce our sanctuary and the beast enter our room? That night felt different from the rest – the screaming was as angry as ever, but there was something else too: something deep and painful. A profound, almost demonic voice slowly repeated the mantra: 'Why? Why? Why?'

With our faces buried under the blankets, we closed our eyes; it was the monster again. The voice moved slowly and with meaning from one room to the next, growing louder with every heavy footstep. We held our breath, hoping the voice wouldn't find us, but it was drawn to us as a mother to a crying baby.

It seemed that our invisibility worked this time. The voice moved away, each twisted word slowly becoming more distant with each breath held. At last we allowed ourselves to relax our tense muscles, and we opened our eyes. 'Are you okay?' I whispered as I peered into the whites of Shell's eyes. She nodded in reply as she slowly released her grip on my hand. 'It's going to be okay, Shell,' I said as I wrapped my arms around her.

We woke to the sound of shouting outside our bedroom window. Immediately the fear returned. 'Is that Mum again?' Shell asked, still too scared to raise her voice above a murmur. I raised myself up onto my elbows just so that my eyes could peek above the window sill. Outside our front gate were the flashing blue lights of an ambulance. The lights appeared to dance around in a circle, occasionally highlighting a woman in the street. My chest tightened as I realised it was Mum. 'It's Mum, isn't it?' came Shell's hushed voice. 'What's happening?'

'Come and look for yourself,' I replied as I shuffled over to make room for Shell at the window. As two pairs of eyes peered down on the scene below, Mum must have sensed an audience. In the glow of the artificial light we could see her standing in the road in her nightgown. As the men in green made their way towards her she turned away and ran. 'They're trying to kill me,' she screamed as her bare feet pounded against the hard tarmac of the road. Dad sprinted after her, leaving two paramedics standing confused and without a patient.

Dad's attempts at recapture must have gone well,

because now the paramedics leaned over Mum's body. She lay supine on the kitchen floor, a knife by her hand and bloody wounds on her wrists. We were good at hiding our fear, and we sat without tears – watching. Dad sat at the kitchen table, his head in his hands. Shell and I sat in the darkened living room, peering from behind the door. If Dad had known we were witness to the drama, he would have ushered us up to bed and told us that everything was okay, but tonight he was totally unaware of anything other than the woman on the floor. Dad had been witness to this scene many times, but that night he was totally consumed by loss. It wasn't just the knowledge that Mum could have died; it was the loss of power, the loss of the family. For the last ten years, he had tried to keep things normal – he'd been the one holding the cracks together – but now he looked beaten, a man struggling to accept the fact that he had lost. A man unable to help the woman he loved.

This was the start: the moment of clarity, of reckoning. It was when I suddenly understood that our family was not a normal family, that Shell and I were not children anymore. Every stolen night, every tear that shouldn't have been – it was all a lie. Shelley and I had thought that this was all how it was supposed to be, that there was no other way. It wasn't Dad's fault; he'd just been trying to protect us from the truth. With every breath, Dad struggled to keep the family afloat, but in that boat we were unaware of the darkness beneath. For every strong stoke that Dad took, the boat sunk a little further; for every bucket of water he tipped out, more raged over the sides. Our little wooden boat belonged deep amongst the rocks below.

Our hearts broke that night – not for Mum, but for Dad. He was the strong one, the glue that held us together. We knew then that it was time for us to outgrow childhood, to help hold Dad up and support him. We knew that Mum would return in a few days and sleep for a week, and when she woke, we would have bacon sandwiches and stay up late – but for this family, it was the end. We'd turned a new corner, finding ourselves without signposts or directions.

* * *

Unfortunately, this time Mum didn't come home. Severalls was the local psychiatric hospital where the desperate were taken. It was a typical psychiatric hospital: a large red-brick building with ornate windows and an entrance shouldered by tall white columns. It was the classic horror-movie building, designed to house the mad and insane: the perfect location for a murder mystery. For two ten-year-olds, it was a place of nightmares, so much so that Dad would not allow us inside to visit, instead thinking it better to lock us in the car, away from the scary people. In fact, he'd leave us in open view of the inmates, who found us an interesting distraction from their own tortured minds. Shell and I sat in the back seat next to each other, staring at the funny people who knocked on the windows and grinned at us. We would sit in silence, not daring to move, not sure what to make of these strangers. Were they friend, foe or just like Mum?

Whilst we sat there one day, trying to categorise the toothless man tapping on the back window of Dad's Ford Escort Estate, a chair came flying through the large, ornate window by the asylum's front door. Mum stood behind the empty frame, screaming. Dad stood to her left, a look of disbelief and dismay on his face, while another man, to Mum's right, hung his head low in a sign of surrender.

We left the premises shortly after, Dad quiet and sombre in the driver's seat. As we drove down the long, gravelled drive that crunched beneath the tyres of the car, a tall, willowy woman with bright-blue eyeshadow jumped in front of the car, daring us to continue. Dad stopped with a shudder and stared at the women. In her hand was a small branch, thick with summer leaves. The woman moved – as quickly and gracefully as a gazelle – to the driver's side of the car and knocked on the window. Dad turned to us and gave a comical, weary smile. We stared back, confused. Dad opened the window.

'This is for you,' the woman said with a full grin.

Dad took the branch, sliding it through the narrow opening of the window. 'Thanks,' he said, and he closed the window sharply.

A short distance from the exit, Dad stopped and threw the unwanted gift from the car. He turned to us and calmly said, 'Well, girls, I would have much preferred a bunch of daffs!'

It was the first time in a long time that we had laughed

– full-blown belly laughs that hurt. Through the laughter, we let go of the tensions of the day. Every laugh that left our bodies was one less sob to leave our hearts.

* * *

The following Saturday, we were allowed to take Mum out to the local park for the afternoon. It was a warm summer's day, and a brass band was playing in the bandstand in the centre of the park. We sat on the grass, eating ice cream, looking like any other family on a day out, and to look at us you would have thought we were a normal family. Mum was attentive – loving, even. She asked about school, and although we had finished school three weeks earlier for the summer, we said it was fine. It felt wonderful but unnatural. The pain in her eyes was evident, and she spoke in a voice that seemed drained of life. Even at the age of ten, I could tell that this wasn't the mum I knew. Her complexion was pale, and her normally dark, full hair lay lank against her cheeks. Her once-loving hazel eyes radiated sadness as they looked past me into a world that we were not party to. Nowadays we would blame it on the drugs and the other barbaric treatments of the day, but I saw only a woman who had accepted her illness and given up the fight. The dark water had taken her; she had decided to stop kicking and had surrendered to the comforting arms of suffocation and darkness in the cold and lonely depths below.

That afternoon, we went boating on the lake – well, Shelley and I did. Mum sat on a bench watching, pretending to see us, whilst Dad stood on the bank, shouting out instructions on how to guide the small canoe around the lake. However much we tried, Shell and I could not direct that boat in the direction we wanted. We paddled around in circles, going left when we meant to go right. When the bell rang to signal the end of our thirty-minute session, Shell and I continued to paddle round and round. We began to get more and more anxious as we struggled to steer the canoe back to the start point. Dad continued to shout instructions but soon lost hope in us suddenly becoming expert sailors – instead, he jumped into the shallow lake. Grabbing hold of the nose of the canoe, he guided us through the water to the pontoon.

Mum didn't seem to notice Dad's soggy trousers and squelching shoes when we returned to the car; she only looked silently at the houses that we passed. She never turned her head to look at us or smile, but remained in the world where she had chosen to stay. Not a word was spoken until we reached the large, ornate doors of the hospital.

'Time to say goodbye to Mummy,' Dad said as he turned to us, sitting in the back. At last Mum turned and smiled at us, apparently seeing us for the first time.

'Bye, Mummy,' we said as we took it in turns to hug her.

'Bye, my angels' – and she left.

* * *

Once home, Dad pensively paced the living room,

appearing to wrestle with a conversation in his head. Shell and I sat on the sofa, watching him, trying to anticipate the words that he was preparing to say, but all that I could think of was how much I hated this sofa. It was a sickly green-leather thing torn with age; the arms were speckled with cigarette burns where Mum had fallen asleep while smoking. Shell and I had to polish that monstrous thing from top to bottom every Saturday with Mr. Sheen to earn our fifty-pence pocket money, and we hated every second. Shell and I now sat on that sofa, so close that our shoulders were tight against one another, our bodies only occupying half a cushion.

Dad stopped pacing and knelt in front of us. His knees cracked as he tried to crouch low enough to meet our eyes. He gently took our hands between his large, muscular fingers. 'It's time to tell you the truth,' he said, casting his eyes down at his knees. 'When Mummy went into the special hospital, the doctors wanted to find out why Mummy gets so sad. They gave Mummy a special medicine that made her remember things – terrible things that happened. These things hurt Mummy very much.' He paused, not knowing what to say. 'Mummy is very unhappy, and it makes her cry a lot.' He continued as he cast his gaze over our faces: 'Grandad and Nanny weren't very nice to her when she was little.' He stopped again, delaying the words that needed to be said. How do you tell two ten-year-olds that their mother was sexually abused by her father – our granddad? That her life had started with unimaginable cruelty and sadness? This would be just one of the unbelievable stories that we would hear as our lives went on. Whether all were true is something I will never know, but the torment these memories caused decided the direction of Mum's life and, to a lesser extent, all our lives. There in front of us was Dad, trying to tell us why we were not a normal family, that our lives were never going to be normal, that our lives were now and forever going to be dominated by our mother's mania.

4

A GAME OF CHESS

I stared at the guppy floating on the top of the water. It lay on its side, one fin sticking up in the air and one blank eye looking back at me. Shell and I were perched on a large brown bag of potatoes in the outside loo, peering over the top of the fish tank. I poked the fish with my index finger, and the bloated body floated away until it hit the opposite side of the tank, where it bounced back to where it started. Guppies are a species of fish that eat their dead, so it wasn't unusual to see a dead guppy with half a fin missing and flesh hanging from its abdomen. Nature has an impressive way of recycling energy, and if that means eating your dead uncle, then so be it.

Shell and I spent a great deal of time in the outside loo, a brick-built appendage attached to the side of the house. While the loo worked fine, it was used mainly as a storage space for old tins of paint and bags of sprouting potatoes. Shell and I would sit on the bag of mouldy potatoes, writing stories and colouring pictures with marker pens. They were usually horror stories – tales of hungry were-wolves killing unsuspecting tourists camping in the wild. The pictures were of stick figures with blood pouring from bites in their necks, or else of people running, terrified, from hungry werewolves resembling cuddly teddy bears with fangs. We would spend the day crafting these pages into books, and once finished we would giggle while reading them, dreaming of the international stars that would appear in the movie adaptations, before hiding the documents in a box under the stairs.

Even at eleven years old, Shell and I were painfully shy. It was difficult for us to form friendships as we were awkward and socially inept with strangers. When faced with a strange face and polite conversation, we would immediately panic, look at the ground and mumble some unintelligible reply. We were so scared of even the briefest human interactions that we would argue about whose turn it was to answer the telephone or the door. If the lady on the till at Tesco said that a box of washing powder cost five hundred pounds, we would panic and apologise for not having the correct amount of money. For most of our young teenage lives, we hid under a veil of shyness, unable to make contact with the outside world. While normal teens walked into town in groups, Shell and I lived in a world of stories and fantasies, where we knew we could decide the endings. In our fantasy worlds, the heroines always conquered and over-came evil.

* * *

Shell and I were best friends – if not for each other, we would each have been incredibly lonely. When I think back to those summer holidays and our shared loneliness, it's hard not to feel sad. Not only did we lack the courage to make friends, but even if we tried, it was too difficult to explain the unusual arrangements of our household. We couldn't have friends come to the house without first confirming the lay of the land. We were constantly on high alert, waiting for intelligence back from our scouting party before daring to move our troops. When Mum returned from the hospital she would spend hours sat pensively on the green sofa, smoking in her nightdress. Her hands would shake as if she was terrified of what she saw, and the tea would spill from the mug she'd balanced precariously on the armrest.

Most days, we'd find her staring at the living-room wall, a horrified look on her face. Other days, Mum would look at us intently as if trying to shake open a box in her mind, and when the lid fell, she would smile, suddenly remembering who we were. On the imperfect days, when the scouting party returned with fallen soldiers, her face would stiffen and her eyes would narrow. As her mouth twisted and hardened, she would stare at the two girls before her. The rage would radiate from those hazel eyes that now were mere inches from our terrified faces. 'You are evil,' she would repeat, hard and slow.

Today we were double-ranked pawns waiting for our

next move. As we moved to our next position, hoping to evade capture, we instantly knew we had made a blunder. The commanding piece stood tall in front of us. 'Where are you going?' she asked. We stood silent, not understanding the true meaning of the question. 'Aren't you going to cook dinner?' Mum said with spitefulness.

'No,' Shell replied, with more courage than I could muster. We made our next move, hoping to make it to the endgame, but the queen had her invisible ranks giving her strength. 'Mum, please, we just want to go upstairs.' Shell stepped to the side without losing eye contact, making her vulnerable to being taken. Mum's eyes followed the pawn, and I could feel the tension build. It was an illegal move that felt like a standoff. The silent battle between them raged, and I knew I had to do something before it exploded. I laid our king down and resigned. I had to move now. I grabbed Shell's arm and pulled her towards me. 'We are going to do our homework, Mum,' I said, and we ran.

I honestly don't think she saw Shell and me that day, but I can imagine the blackness she felt. An image of her father, maybe – or was it some manifestation of everything she wasn't or couldn't be?

A few hours later we returned to find Mum back on the sofa, watching the demons again. After confirming there were no smouldering embers from her cigarette about to burn a hole in Mum's flannelette nightie, we started to peel potatoes and carrots for tea. It was then time to tackle the frozen wasteland that was the freezer. We placed mind over matter as we negotiated our way past bags of forgotten peas to the sausages that had become embedded in the iceberg at the rear. Fortunately, by the time Dad had got home from work, we had discarded the burnt tea towel in the dustbin and vanquished the smell of smoke and burnt oil from the mild chip-pan fire, and we presented him with an acceptable-tasting dinner of sausage and chips. On one similar occasion, Shell and I tried to make a french onion soup from the leftover vegetables edging past their best in the bottom of the fridge. It was so bad that we nicknamed it 'the mother-in-law destructor.' Culinary skill did not come easily to us, but we endeavoured to play our parts, with minor triumphs remembered and small fires forgotten.

* * *

It was summer 1981, the year that Shell and I were preparing for secondary school. As a family, we had settled into a routine, and Shell and I had become increasingly responsible for household chores, cooking and looking after Mum while Dad was at work. Dad did his utmost, but he was beginning to find the everyday uphill anxieties harder and harder to manage. He appeared continually exhausted; his hair became unkempt and his clothes old and torn. Aside from a few rare moments of joy, the sun had left his eyes, and the hole in his heart was now visible and without protection.

We would wake early on Saturdays to an empty, quiet house. The daylight that escaped from the edges of the closed curtains emphasised the intricate swirls of hazy cigarette smoke, which danced in the air from the previous night. The darkness of the living room would remain as Shell and I spent the morning watching children's TV, eating sweet-and-sour pot noodles for breakfast and laughing at the men running around without direction in bright-yellow banana suits. The pot noodles were our favourite, but even today I can't face the small sachet of soy sauce without thinking of the mashed-up beetle blood that Shell told me it contained. If it had been a quiet night, Mum would appear in the afternoon, wearing a large, baggy dress that resembled a flowery blue parachute. There is a photo of Mum in that very dress leaning up against Dad's Ford Escort Estate. She appears to be looking down, her hands on her hips, like a mafia boss about to pass sentence on some poor employee who has dishonoured the family.

That day, Mum bounced on her feet and asked if we would like breakfast. We didn't like to tell her that it was three p.m. and we were filled with salty synthetic noodles and crushed beetle blood, so we indulged in ham rolls and Monster Munch crisps, which lifted her mood even more. We went shopping in the local town centre – not that there was much to envy there. The one and only clothes shop had only a small array of items, but Shell and I returned home with matching penguin jumpers, mine a deep blue and Shell's a bright blood-red. Large penguins occupied the entire fronts of our jumpers, long wool scarves around their necks. They were thick and warm – I guess that's why they were so cheap to buy in July. We also returned with white plastic gladiator sandals, the number-one fashion accessory of the moment! They were stiff with cheapness and rubbed the skin from our toes, but they would raise our profiles in the fashion world. That summer, we would wear them through sunshine and rainstorms, even when the water entered the slots between the straps and our feet would slide about on the plastic soles. We would smile, feeling that we were normal, just another pair of eleven-year-old girls on their summer holidays with blisters on their feet.

The following morning, the dark clouds descended, and the flowery parachute was replaced by the nightgown pocked with cigarette holes. It had been an unsettling night of anguished cries and screams, and Mum had not left the living room. The entire house had been awake much of the night, and Dad had reluctantly left for work tired and guilt-ridden. As a self-employed carpenter, he had little choice but to leave us; if he didn't work, he didn't get paid. As a family, we had little money, and when Mum was on a high she would spend the little spare money we had, forfeiting the week's groceries for a day's outing or a trip to the hairdresser. Dad left comforted by the knowledge that eventually Mum would fall into a deep drug-induced sleep and we would spend the day entertaining ourselves in the relative safety of our bedrooms.

When Dad returned home, he reluctantly opened the back door and peered through the small gap, gauging the atmosphere of the house without commitment. He could never be totally sure what to expect, so a cautious entry was mandatory. He smiled brightly as he found Shell and me watching TV happily in the living room – Mum was still in the throes of the chemically induced sleep. The mood was light and electric, and the anxieties of what the night might have brought were forgotten. We played Monopoly, just the three of us. Dad was always the boot; he pretended not to see our characters land on his Mayfair hotels, and he sneaked extra cash onto our dwindling piles. Eventually, the lack of sleep forced us to bed, and Dad kissed and held us tightly in a silent plea for forgiveness.

* * *

Again, we woke to the sounds of sobbing. The echo of breaking glass vibrated from the room below. We stayed in bed, not daring to move, and I tried without success to stop the pounding in my chest. We shut our eyes as the bedroom door slammed open. Footsteps rang out – one, then another, then another, the floorboards quaking beneath their weight. I felt the breath on my cheek and tightened the lids over my eyes, hoping to block out the sound.

'Girls, wake up.'

The soft but desperate voice broke my trance.

'Lee, Shell – wake up and get dressed.' Dad leaned over us, so close I could almost feel the prickle of his moustache on my face.

'Dad, why? What's going on?'

'Just get up and get some warm clothes on as fast as you can,' he said, peering into our quizzical faces and horrified eyes. 'Don't worry, we just need to leave for tonight. We will be back in the morning.'

At that moment, a haunting voice screamed, 'You fucking liars,' and I knew at once why we had to leave. We quickly dressed in jeans and jumpers and fled towards the work van parked outside. Through the open living-room door I could see Mum frantically moving across the living room wall, a marker pen in her hand. The familiar cream walls were now soiled with bizarre dark markings. I focused on the wall, and the words appeared: *Liar. Bastards. Killing me.*

The coffee table stood awkwardly on its side and the lamp lay broken at its feet. On the TV unit stood a highball glass filled with thick, dark coffee, and a lightbulb sat on top. She turned, seeing us for the first time. 'Go on then, run away,' she hissed, hatred seeping from every syllable. As her eyes bore into ours, we turned and fled.

* * *

Dad turned the key in the ignition, and a low whine rose. The engine seemed to cough, a slow mechanical expulsion of air that rolled into silence. Panic swept through the van.

'Dad,' Shell said quickly, 'we have to go.'

The slow whine echoed through the van once more. As the electrical signals sparked the ignition, the engine roared with the same anxiety as the people that occupied it. Beside me, Shell started shrieking and pointing towards the house. 'Dad! Go now! Go now!' Tears were rolling down her face.

Both Dad and I at once turned towards the front door.

The door hung from its hinges. On the doorstep stood a

monster – it looked like Mum, but it wasn't her. The being that loomed from the shadows of our home was a demon who threw herself forwards with a resolve born of damnable hatred.

'*Dad!*' Shell and I screamed at once, terror oozing from our every pore. The knife in Mum's hand glinted in the moonlight as she flew in silence down the concrete path, the whites of her eyes wide and awful.

The van moved with the power and will of three desperate humans, and we fled.

'What do we do now?' I asked Dad as the gentle rumble of the engine hid my sobs. The van stood idle in a lay-by about twenty minutes from home. I watched the lorry drivers standing around a van selling hot food and tea, and I wondered what it must feel like to have a normal life. There was a pause before Dad opened his door and jogged towards the van. He returned with three bacon sandwiches and tea and we began to eat in silence, without facing the question, *What next?* It was not long before there was an air of calm that settled between us, and I managed a smile as I devoured my food.

'Well, I've just spent the money I had in my pocket, so how do you feel about sleeping in the van tonight? It will be like camping.'

Shell and I looked at each other and smiled. 'Okay!' we replied, half excited about sleeping in the van and half relieved that we didn't have to go home.

The sun was just lifting its nose above the horizon when the van came to a stop outside our house. Not a word was said as we gently closed the van doors behind us. I could feel the apprehension and rising anxiety ooze from Dad as we neared the front door. Shell and I shuffled behind Dad, using his large frame as a shield. The house stood broken but silent as we passed through the shattered rim of the door and into the front room. All at once we released the breath that we held and the tension in our bodies. Mum was asleep, and the monster lay quiet for now.

The morning brought just another day at school for Shell and me. We became well rehearsed at hiding the anxieties of the previous night, and our acting skills flourished as the years progressed. It was another day in the life of our family. While our friends wished for late bedtimes and ice cream, Shell and I wished for a peaceful night in our own beds.

* * *

Over the next few days Mum's dark mood lifted, and we all lifted with her. All four of us rode on Mum's emotions, and we would soar in and out on waves of endorphins, savouring those rare and dizzying highs. Once, we stood under an overflowing drain pipe in the torrential rain until we were sodden, not caring what passers-by thought. Other times, Dad reinvented himself as Tommy Cooper by placing the dorsum of his hand under our chins and reciting 'Get out of that' in a rough East End accent. These were the moments that made us feel normal. These pinpricks of hope would encourage us to endure, to continue until the cycle resumed.

* * *

We didn't talk about mental health when I was growing up. It was a clandestine subject that even doctors turned away from, in part because they didn't wholly understand it and in part because it just wasn't 'sexy' to specialise in. No one got awards for their outstanding contributions to understanding mental illness. We had many visitors to the house, each with their own approach and each promising a cure. These people ranged from neighbours bearing shepherd's pies to clergymen offering prayer. And then there were the medical treatments: Mum tried them all. First, the so-called 'truth drug' sodium thiopental, a chemical that depresses and calms anxiety. It induces drowsiness and dulls inhibitions, allowing the victim to speak freely without the fear of reprisal. While spies in James Bond films were attempting to extract secrets, psychiatrists were forcing memories from the mind of my mum. In moments of confusion and disorientation, Mum began to reveal hidden and inconceivable truths from her childhood.

Bringing reality to the forefront of Mum's memory resulted in a psychotic episode and, eventually, a breakdown. After weeks in the psychiatric hospital, the doctors decided that the 'last-resort' treatment of electroconvulsive therapy (ECT) was the way to go. To me, ECT represents all that is wrong with how we treat mental illness; it's a barbaric act, and it is still performed today. When the electric current passes through the brain, the body reacts by entering an epileptic state. Theoretically, this causes neural pathways to rewire, which hopefully results in a positively reshaped brain and the erasure of errant behaviours. ECT conjures images from old black-and-white horror films where the mad scientist places electrodes on each temple while the assistant forces a cloth between the teeth of the bound victim. Lightning strikes outside the window, and the crazy, haunting laugh echoes and rebounds around the old brick laboratory as life enters the monster below.

The ECT worked for a while but in the end the doctors eventually settled on a cocktail of mind-altering drugs that were served daily with each meal. There were uppers to lift her mood, downers to control the unpredictable swing of emotions, anti-psychotic pills to stop the paranoia and delusions and finally the tablets that just numbed it all, quietening the conscience and allowing sleep to overcome the torment. These drugs worked, I suppose, but they also extinguished what little thought and drive Mum had left – they wiped out what little was left of the woman Mum had once been.

These drugs wiped out Mum's suicidal intentions and calmed her tormented mind, but at what cost? Is it better to live a tormented life or no life at all? Is it better to live as a monster or to die as a human? At the time, I don't think anyone really cared. As long as the monster was quiet and smiling, it didn't really matter what the human was saying.

Behind every mentally ill person is a family in crisis,

unknown, hidden and forgotten. Back then, there were no treatments or support programs for the families of the ill, and it was those silent voices that were left to swallow and absorb the fallout. When I was sixteen, a mental health nurse told me that I should be more supportive of Mum. At the time, I thought she was right – I'd let Mum down, and her pain was my fault. I now think back on the memory with anger and frustration. If only that nurse could have seen the suffering that stood in front of her, if only she could have heard the silent pleas for help, if only she knew the hours spent convincing Mum not to overdose or to slit her wrists – if only she knew.

5

SITTING UNDER A WATERFALL OF SKELETONS

The nausea rose in my throat, and the chocolate cake felt suddenly heavy and rotten on my tongue. The thought of the calories entering my body was too painful to entertain, so I bit down hard on the loose skin of my hand. With every mouthful I could feel the fat lining my body, causing it to expand and swell. It felt as though the cake was creeping under my skin like a spider, antagonising every nerve that it touched.

We sat on deck chairs in the overgrown grass of the back garden. A large double mattress was leaned up against the shed behind us. Mum had fallen asleep while smoking again, and the bed had been dragged out into the garden in the middle of the night so the fire could be extinguished. It was a hot day, and I had smothered suntan lotion over my legs, believing that the more lotion you applied, the quicker you would tan. Mum had given us each a large portion of shop-bought cake, covered in double cream and served in a blue cereal bowl. It was one of those days when Mum would try to atone for all the meals she didn't make us, resulting in an abundant array of foods, thick with fat and artificial ingredients.

I studied the iceberg of stodgy brown mess surrounded by the sea of cream. I moved it slowly around the bowl with my spoon, surreptitiously letting a portion fall to the ground. The dog swallowed it seemingly without even opening her mouth, unaware of the sugar rush that was about to hit. I cleared my dinner without eating even a quarter of it and smiled happily, knowing that I had not only fooled everyone but also asserted control over my own body.

I was around twelve when I started to starve myself. It wasn't a desire to be thin; it was a desire to have control. My life had no order, no structure – every action, thought and feeling was dominated by Mum and her illness, and we were forced to relinquish all that we were. The one thing that no one else could control was my inner body. Only I could command what happened; only I could write the conclusion to its story.

This began my twisted and tangled relationship with food. I hated it, but it occupied my every waking second. I was obsessed by its power over me, how it dictated every move that I made. I craved its constant attention, but when faced with it, I would push it away like an unwanted lover. Food was master and slave, and though I felt in control, I was anything but. Food was my enemy – my master – and anorexia was the battlefield on which we fought.

My tortuous dance with dieting was easily hidden. For three years, my inner battle went undetected, overlooked in favour of Mum's illness. I hid my skinny frame under baggy jumpers, and my dinners slipped unnoticed into the bin or the dog's bowl. I would often feel weak and lifeless, able to summon just enough energy to curl in front of the gas fire in the living room, which never emitted enough heat to warm my freezing body. My periods stopped and my hair began to thin, but nobody seemed to notice. Every pound I lost was a triumph, and the joy of achievement was addictive.

Over time, I became sneaky and self-absorbed, only caring about myself, my food and how fat I looked. Although the clothes hung loosely from my bony frame, all I saw was white, flabby flesh rolling beneath my school shirts. I became a feeder: I would plan and cook large, elaborate meals of cheese-filled lasagne or pastry-covered pies. I would serve Dad and Shell large portions, becoming distressed if they couldn't clear their plates. Mum had her own eating routine. She ate at odd times throughout the day and night and, when the mood or medication allowed, she could consume large amounts of food, sometimes engulfing an entire swiss roll without even pausing for breath.

As Shell started to hide her expanding waist under baggy jumpers, I revelled in the sight of my hip bones protruding and the ever-enlarging gap between my thighs. I wanted everyone to see my success, to know what I had achieved, so I started to wear tight-fitting clothes. When I was around fourteen, there was little money for clothes. What little we did have was controlled by Mum, so Shell and I had little choice over our wardrobe, meaning we each possessed a small collection of jeans, jumpers and the occasional knee-length dress. With no instruction or knowledge, I tried to craft my own dress from an old 1970s curtain. It was thick polyester, white with an orange-and-brown floral design – the most hideous material imaginable! I clumsily drew a dress shape on the reverse side of the curtain and used the near-blunt kitchen scissors to cut around the slim line and short hem of the design. Over the next hour, I used a running stitch to bind it together, getting excited as it neared completion. When at last I studied the finished article, I realised that I had forgotten one important aspect of a functioning garment: a way into it. In my excitement, I'd forgotten zips or buttons – there was only enough space in the top for my head.

As I became consumed with control, I failed to recognise (or was unwilling to accept) the change in Shell. Unable to find an escape of her own, my twin fell into the shadows of the forgotten. She detached from the family, spending hours hiding beneath jumpers and heavy books in her room. At meal times, she would appear in the kitchen door, her fringe in her eyes and the roll-neck jumper covering her mouth. The loneliness she felt must have been overwhelming – she was a teenage girl in crisis, with only her books to confide in. As anorexia gripped me, loneliness took hold of Shell. We were two sisters bound by the same shores but now oceans apart. At nineteen, Shell would face her own battle with bulimia.

I was slowly losing the battle over my body and mind. Becoming increasingly ill, I found my anorexia more and more difficult to hide from my family. I would often faint without reason, waking with my hands tightly gripping my arms, preventing me from crumpling to the floor. It is true what they say: your hearing really is the last sense to go. I remember that when the blackness covered my eyes and the strength left my legs, I would still hear the sounds of the life that spun around me. Words would be muffled and the light would flicker in and out, but I could hear the anxiety in the voices of those around me as they debated what to do with the fainting girl.

* * *

As the once-lush green leaves turned differing shades of yellow and brown, the autumn signalled the return to secondary school. It was a time of mixed anxieties; not only were we worried about new teachers and friendships, but Shell and I also had to worry about our webs of explanations and lies. On the first day of term, Shell and I entered through the gates of the large secondary modern in our starched and slightly oversized uniforms, our expectations inflated and a faint optimism hanging over our shoulders. We were students who managed to keep under the radar, never under- or over-achieving and adept at evading teachers and adults. It was easy to stay quiet in the overpopulated classroom, easy to always hand in average homework, easy to remain invisible.

While Shell started to excel academically, I struggled to keep up. I found that the numbers on the page never added up and the letters played tricks on me by jumping out of place. I found solace in running fast. I was good for a while, until anorexia said no more. The two dry Ryvitas at lunch were not enough to placate the starvation my body faced, nor were they enough to provide the energy needed. I hated anorexia for that; it robbed me of the one thing that I could do, that I felt proud of. It gave me control over my body, but on the other hand it stole from me. It was a con man who promised me release and retribution, but who then showed up at my door demanding payment. I was stranded, alone with nothing but an empty promise and a neglected body.

I lay next to the painted white lines with my heart pounding so hard I couldn't catch my breath. The muscles in my legs were burning as the lactic acid rose, cramping them. I had just finished my first hundred-metre race of the year, and my body was rebelling against me. I rolled onto my side as my breathing settled and smelt for the first time the sweetness of the newly cut grass. The nausea was passing, and the darkness was fading with every deep breath as oxygen rushed to my exhausted muscles and starved brain. I opened my heavy eyes to see my PE teacher, Miss Holloway, looking directly at me. 'It's really biting now, isn't it?' she said before turning and walking away.

I couldn't hide it anymore. My control was being exposed for what it was. The power I had over my body was lost, and now I realised at once that I had failed. Anorexia now held dominion, dictating how I looked and what I did and showing the world the weak, pathetic girl I had become.

* * *

I sat in the deck chair in front of yet another burnt mattress. The newly mowed grass revealed dead, yellow roots beneath. It was getting late, and the thought of eating a meal was stomach-churning, but in my mind, I knew that I had little choice if I wanted things to change. The alternative was to perish, and I wasn't prepared for that, at least not yet. I didn't know how to come back from this life I'd created for myself, but I knew that it had begun to destroy the only thing I had left: my will to live. Anorexia had left me alone, devoid of the companionship I'd believed it would bring, with only a defeated mind and a protruding skeleton to call my own.

Soon, the emotional turmoil turned to physical pain. Pangs of agony shot down my legs and back like electrical pulses, causing me to whimper and weep. As I frantically rubbed my legs, hoping to fool the nerve endings into thinking that the pain had stopped, I became aware that Dad was now sitting beside me. He wasn't looking at me; his gaze was fixed on the yellowing grass at his feet.

'Dad? What's wrong?'

He remained silent.

'Dad?'

He hesitated, the words hovering in the air above him, still unspoken.

'She had an affair,' he said at last. His voice was flat and cold.

'Who?'

'Your mum. The last time she was in hospital, she had an affair with another patient.'

The words stuck in my ears. My vocal cords tangled, the fibres vibrating but not forming a response.

'She didn't want to come home at first and refused to leave.'

Still, words would not leave my mouth.

Dad grew quiet, his stare still fixed on his feet. That was the only time he mentioned the affair – he never spoke of it again.

'Lee,' he said at last, 'please get well. I don't want to lose you too.'

If there was ever a pivotal moment that spun every molecule in my body, that rendered me condemnable and inexpiable, it was this moment. He broke, tears falling without hindrance or embarrassment. They flooded through me in waves of despair that washed every selfish cell from me in torrents of regret and remorse. What had I done? Anorexia had not only extinguished me – it had asserted its devastating power over Dad and Shell too. In my own isolated world, I had been blind to the suffering that I had caused to the two people that I cared for most of all. They had been witnesses to my self-destruction, lacking any influence or power to change the path that I had designed for myself. They had stood in the shadows, watching me starve, pleading with me to ignore the Trojan horse that was anorexia.

As I sat on the ground, holding Dad tighter than I had ever held anything before, I silently vowed that I wouldn't let this illness dictate the end of my story. It could be retold and reworded; it didn't have to end this way. As our anguished cries silenced, I made a promise that I still strive to uphold today – for anorexia never completely leaves. I made the promise to get better and never let it return.

* * *

In the eighties, anorexia was known about but was poorly understood. I desperately wanted to be well, to overcome this part of life that had become all-consuming. There were no websites, no chatrooms and no workshops; the only help I could access was from my general practitioner. As I sat in front of him, not knowing what to say, he proclaimed that I was underweight at just six stone. Anorexia was silently dancing on my shoulder, and I knew that it was winning; I was still losing weight and finding it impossible to pass the starting line. After three years of this life, how could I step over the line? All I wanted was for the doctor to tell me how I could begin, how I could leave the starting blocks and release the chains that held me.

The GP sat before me, bewildered, and I could sense that he was struggling for words. He took a breath and sighed. 'Do you have a boyfriend?' he asked.

So, I thought, *I'm on my own.*

* * *

When you are out running and you start to feel the tiredness biting at your heels and the burn in your muscles, it takes determination and belief to continue to the finish. You hear runners say that if you are faced with a hill in front of you, you should concentrate on the top and not look down. That, sadly, is not wisdom that can be applied to the fight against anorexia.

When I looked ahead, I could see every dip, crack and bump I would have to pass before reaching the top. I learned instead to look at the ground as I ran, taking one stride at a time. If I were to see all the fences at once, I would crumble, unable to face what stretched before me. Of course, running in this way would result in more than a few falls – but I became adept at picking myself up off the floor, brushing the dust off my running leggings and starting again.

It took ten years to reach the top of my hill, and I had my fair share of bruises, cuts and scars to show for it. Unbeknownst to me, I'd not run that race alone. Once I found the courage to pass the starting line, Dad and Shell came to run beside me. They would shout encouragement as I stumbled, and although they could not physically pick me up from the ground, they mentally urged me on. Once again, my life was saved.

6

POTATOES ON THE LAWN

There was a time when things were calm. I was still fighting my diet demons, Shell was still battling loneliness and Dad was continually resisting the wolf at the door. Mum and the illness still commanded centre stage, and the rest of us were still watching from the wings. It was everyday life for us, and a good day was one without incident. It was a time of routine, however odd the routine may have been, and we became accustomed to our habits and rituals. Of course, this calm wouldn't last long. The cracks soon appeared at our feet, and we were unsure whether we should step right over the gap or allow ourselves to be engulfed by it.

Shell and I were around sixteen and sitting in the garden when the boiling water sprayed past our faces. A heap of uncooked potatoes landed on the grass nearby, the pan upended. Apparently, dinner was served.

Mum was at the back door, staring at us with that

hateful look in her eyes that we knew so well. 'Fucking dinner!' she screamed. Shell and I stared at the still-steaming potatoes lying desolate and lonely at our feet. Today was not going to be a good day. On any other day, Mum would pay no attention to the dinner we had cooked or the washing we'd hung on the line, but today it enraged her. Perhaps she resented the fact that Shell and I were coping with the everyday chores, or perhaps she felt that we were taking control somehow, hammering home the fact that she was no longer needed. She stood at the door with triumph in her eyes, staring us down before retreating to the kitchen. The anger and rage suddenly swelled within me, and every muscle in my body began to twitch. Without thinking, I rose from my knees and walked with blind purpose to the kitchen, where Mum stood over the now-empty hob.

'What the hell are you doing?' I shouted, the words pouring from me before I could stop them.

'It's all your fault,' she spat, emphasising every syllable. 'You are evil. That's why your Dad doesn't love me.'

Before I could restrain myself, my hands tightened into fists around the dinner plate I didn't realise I was holding. Mum looked at me with pure hatred in her eyes, and I could feel the cold that seemed to radiate from her. It burrowed into my mind, and I felt her bitterness and disgust settle deep within. The anger boiled and grew, and before I knew what my arms were doing, the plate came crashing down against the kitchen worktop. The porcelain pieces flew, glinting like diamonds in the air between us before coming to rest. I only wish my anger found such an easy resting place.

Mum and I stood in silence, not knowing what my sudden rebellion meant or what was to come next. In one sharp movement, Mum lunged, grabbing a knife that sat on the kitchen counter. Slowly and with an almost quiet grace, she waved the blade back and forth just inches from my nose. The static in the air suddenly froze, and I heard Mum's deep, quick breaths in the silence.

The blade jerked suddenly, and Mum stepped backwards, her eyes widening. I finally exhaled. Still holding the knife in her hand, she swiftly sidestepped me and ran up the stairs to the bathroom. I looked at Shell, who had appeared beside me in the kitchen. Without exchanging words but in shared silent alarm, Shell and I frantically raced up the stairs, taking two steps at a time.

'Mum, no!' we both screamed as we reached the threshold of the bathroom. Mum stood over the sink, the knife poised above her left wrist, blood already running down between her fingers and under her nails, her breath held taut. She looked at us and frowned. Not a word was uttered, and the silence crackled between us. Mum broke our gaze and moved her eyes back to the knife hovering above her bloody wrist.

'Let me die,' she said calmly.

'Mum, please stop,' I said quietly. I stepped towards her. Her body froze, and she recoiled like a startled deer. The knife halted its journey before dropping with a deafening rattle into the sink. I peered down at the wisps of blood still circling the drain, and Mum threw herself forwards, her fist cannoning towards my face – but I felt nothing. Instead, Mum's fist collided with Shell's cheek, sending her sprawling. Shell had seen what I'd not, and she had stepped in to block the blow. As Mum pushed past us, making her escape, Shell grabbed the collar of her nightgown, pulling her back into the bathroom. With anger fuelling her strength, Mum pulled backwards, dragging Shell with her until she teetered at the top of the stairs. Two bodies paused, one holding the other, two pairs of eyes daring the other to make the next move. The hard, rapid breaths spoke a foreign language understood only by Shell and Mum. Suddenly, Shell released her grip. Mum staggered and slipped, her balance gone, her feet lagging behind her shoulders and hands – but found the stabilising presence of the wall. Her fall broken, she regained her balance and paused. With a final look, Mum stood tall before turning and disappearing down the stairs. I knew where she was going: the kitchen, where the comfort of bottled chemicals would wipe the day clean.

* * *

We sat on the curb, the sun warming our backs. Mum was now confined to her bed, a bandage firmly wound around her wrist. It hadn't taken long to calm her, and an extra cocktail of drugs had rendered her unconscious within minutes. Shell and I doodled on the pavement, drawing patterns with a sharp stone, an easy distraction from the thoughts that ran wild through our heads. A serene numbness settled over us. To any passer-by, we were simply two teenage girls hanging around, trying to occupy the time until Mum called us home for dinner. I glanced at Shell. Her cheek was now starting to swell, and a blush of pale purple was blossoming. She paid no attention to it, choosing instead to concentrate on the intricate swirls of the pattern she was crafting. Still we sat in silence, choosing not to recount the moments we had just endured. As always, we communicated through our common bond, our sisterhood allowing us to comfort one another through silence alone.

The Ford Escort Estate pulled alongside the curb, bumping a wheel as it stopped. Shell and I stayed where we were, not moving our feet, which stretched out on the road in front of the now-stationary vehicle. Dad stepped from the car, finding us amongst the collage of patterns we'd created, and approached us with a huge smile on his face. As he neared, the sparkle of his piercing blue eyes dimmed and the heaviness returned to his step.

'It's okay, Dad,' Shell said. 'Mum's asleep now.'

Dad paused just inches from us, his eyes hardening as they fell upon Shell's face. Without speaking, he knew exactly what had happened. Our eyes followed the six-foot figure as he disappeared up the front garden path to the gate that shielded the rear garden. Shell and I stayed where we were, not daring to follow, knowing what was about to happen. We sat, waiting for the screaming to begin, but the house remained still.

Within minutes, Dad reappeared at the gate, carrying two overstuffed bags. His pace was quick, and every step rang with determination and purpose.

'Okay girls,' he said calmly, 'up you get.'

Shell and I stood and started towards the car, but instead of loading the bags into the boot, Dad turned and headed across the road to the neighbours' house. We followed in silence, confused. It was a school night – normally we would spend the night in the car, returning early the next morning to get dressed and washed before Dad dropped us off at the school gates. If Mum didn't explode until late at night, we'd instead be dropped off at Nana's or Auntie Jean's house, where we'd spend a few days away from the enduring madness. Dad's determination and composure unsettled us on this night, but still we remained silent as we sat nestled together on Jill's sofa. I could feel the pounding of Shell's heart against my shoulder, and mine joined the powerful rhythm, drumming out the suppressed cries we both held inside.

After a few minutes conversing with Jill in her kitchen, Dad reappeared and sat beside us, his hands rubbing his exhausted eyes. Perhaps he was trying to still his own pounding heart. It took another few minutes for him to find the courage – or maybe just the right words – to explain what he had decided.

'I am so sorry, girls. I should not have allowed this to

happen.' Dad paused, his jaw set. 'I will not let your mum hurt you again.' He no longer looked at us – his flashing eyes were fixed on the floor. 'I will not let it happen again,' he repeated, speaking more to himself than to the two girls sitting motionless next to him. In one coordinated motion, Shell and I held Dad, and we silently wept.

* * *

We settled quickly into our new surroundings and routine. Shell and I shared a double bed in Jill's spare room, and Dad crammed his long legs onto the sofa in a ritual of sleep-less nights. To leave Mum and take Shell and me with him must have been the easiest but most terrifying choice for a father to make, and I know that the guilt that he carried weighed on him. Whether we'd communicated it or not, we had all made the decision that we could not continue with the life Mum's illness had forged for us. Dad could absorb the violence that was hurled his way, but he would not tolerate it directed at his girls.

For Shell and me, the sense of relief sat awkwardly alongside guilt. Things were easier now, but with that ease came uncertainty – the future spun on its axis, sending us off on a different trajectory, a path with no marked exits. We had to learn to think differently, to fight against a mindset that the illness had installed. We needed to decide what happened next. We knew that if we returned home, we would not be met with forgiveness or melancholy; there would be no sudden epiphany that we'd been wronged, no repentant Mum apologising for every painful word or action she'd inflicted on us. We were in limbo, with nothing but two hastily packed bags of clothes – we'd left behind toothbrushes and shoes – and a small red hotel on Mayfair.

After school, I would sit at the front-room window, studying the house where I used to live. I sat, shielded from view by the white lace curtain, and peered out at the strange yet familiar building. It seemed to have distorted and altered during the two weeks that had passed since we left. The grass in the front garden was no longer yellow – instead, it was a beautiful spring green. Beyond, the curtained windows appeared lifeless and still, and the sun highlighted the vivid oranges of the pattern. I imagined the dogs, Zoe and Bonnie, curled in their basket. Bonnie, the Jack Russell, would sit balanced upon Zoe's back with her back legs spread comically on either side. I worried that they were missing us and the cuddles that we constantly inflicted upon them. With a start, I realised that the guppies would now be floating, lifeless and wide-eyed, on the surface of the fish tank.

It was a place of uncertainty and anxiety, but it had been our home for the last sixteen years. It had given Shell and me the lives we'd grown accustomed to, and it was the stuff of our childhood memories. We were now dislodged from those lives, and the feeling of displacement kept us on edge. We spent every day doing the normal things – going to school, eating, sleeping – but there was an apprehension and nervousness in every motion we made. Our neighbours were kind, and they made us feel welcome and as comfortable as their three-bedroom semi-detached house would allow. Shell and I helped with everyday tasks such as washing and cooking, but this inevitably ended in potatoes burnt to the bottoms of pans and a lot of pink underwear; we were soon demoted to cleaners.

As time passed, it became more difficult to conceal our usual rituals and habits – God knows, our normal family routine was a far cry from that of the fully functioning family that now watched us. My eating disorder was the most difficult to hide, as the gigantic meals Jill cooked dominated the large kitchen table where the entire family would gather every dinner time for mounds of pasta, bread, and homemade Victoria sponge. I was aware of Jill's constant gaze – she watched every mouthful I took, noting how much of it I ate and how much I passed onto Shell or Dad, until soon I was forcing every sickening mouthful into my unwilling mouth. The conversation and laughter felt unfamiliar, just as alien as the family that sat at the table discussing mundane and normal lives. I sat in awe of what other families would describe as another boring mealtime.

On occasion, Jill was successful in encouraging Shell to leave the bedroom, and we would nervously sit with the family, struggling to join the conversation and activities of a normal, functioning family. Dad displayed the biggest change – he became relaxed and almost jovial. He would stay up late, talking and drinking with Jill's husband, Recco, laughing loudly at jokes that we could never quite hear. Shell and I were unsure of how to feel; it was unnerving to hear Dad, whom we knew as a sombre man, so happy. The stranger in the front room smiled, laughed and cracked jokes, making his audience laugh with him. Though we didn't know it at the time, Dad was turning back into the man he used to be.

7

SEA SERPENTS WEARING GOLD RINGS

It glided and slithered amongst the undulating mounds of sand, its paddle-like tail moving swiftly back and forth in smooth lateral motions. It left its habitat in the dark, hidden depths of the drift lanes deep at the bottom of the ocean. Its eyes were small and black, and its nostrils flared as it hunted. Its sensitive olfactory senses encouraged the forked tongue to protrude, allowing it to taste the presence of its prey. It needed to feed, its greed overpowering the natural drive to stay hidden. The venom was painless, the prey unaware even that the snake's teeth were still embedded in the wound. The muscles that controlled the expansion and relaxation of the prey's lungs slowly halted. It died a slow, suffocating death.

The man relaxed, allowing the back of the chair to take his weight. His hands lay clasped across his chest, and the gold from his ring glinted in the sunlight that streamed through the small and only window. His slightly snug cream suit contrasted with his post-holiday tan, which in turn exaggerated the overly white teeth framed by an exaggerated, patronising grin.

We sat in the small, cramped office, all three of us packed into three small chairs in front of an overly busy desk. The man sat on the opposite side, the desk protecting him from the desperate and odd-looking family who watched him in silence. He inspected us, his eyes tracing our faces.

'Have you rented before?' he asked, leaning forwards, his chair creaking.

'We rented a council house at the top of town, but now my wife will be living there.'

He scanned our faces again, his eyebrows now furrowed in silent question. He took a deep breath through his nose, releasing a quiet, irritating whistle.

'Look!' Dad said in exasperation. 'We need somewhere to live, now rather than later, so is your flat available or not?'

Again, the man leaned back in his chair. 'It is only a one bedroom, you know,' he sneered at last.

'Yes, I am aware of that,' Dad replied, trying to disguise his rising temper. 'If we do rent your flat, I will partition off the bedroom to create two. It's a temporary solution until we can find a more suitable place.' His words were losing their composure, his breaths deepening.

As if the man felt the impending detonation, he stood from his chair.

'Let's see if the flat is available now, shall we? You must

pay the deposit today.' He grinned once again, flashing overly polished teeth that for a moment I felt like knocking from his arrogant smile. When he had left the office to gather paperwork, I looked at Dad, who was looking at Shell, who now turned to look at me.

'Let's just go, Dad,' I said. 'I can't stand it in here any longer.'

We walked out of the office and onto the street without even offering a goodbye.

'Twat,' Dad said, making me smile.

'Arsehole,' I said.

'Wanker.'

'Shelley Morris!' both Dad and I exclaimed together, allowing a burst of laughter to suddenly leave our tense bodies. We returned to the car, still laughing, and made our way back to the neighbours' house. Our search would go on.

* * *

It took another few weeks to find an estate agent without brilliant white teeth and a forked tongue, and we moved into the three-bedroom flat above the said estate agent's shop a month later. It was an exciting time, and we were filled with anticipation, daring for the first time to hope for a different future, a future we'd never thought we'd see – one that was unwritten, uncontrollable by mental illness. Our imagined utopia created castles in the sky for us to dream about.

There was lightness in the air, and the sun that broke through the clouds seemed to sing to me. Even if the rain began to pelt against my face and the cold made my skin pale and shiver, my hope would not be dulled. All three of us began to imagine happiness, a life without constant fear – but behind it all was an endless, sunken foundation of guilt. Our optimism was selfish. To leave Mum behind was unfair, neglectful. Did I have the right to leave my God-given life behind, to try to find contentment without Mum in my life? She was, after all, my mum – my family – and she sat heavily upon my conscience, keeping me from sleep during long nights of regret.

During this time, Dad continued to visit and support Mum, often returning with missing shoes and toothbrushes. Apparently, Mum was uncharacteristically calm and seemed accepting of the situation, which added to our unease.

It came during the night, not long before we were due to move into our new flat. We woke to the sound of screaming outside our window. Something was being thrown at the windows, and the *thud, thud, thud* of the impact seemed to shake the entire house. The household quickly became alive, every person jumping from their sleep, suddenly on guard. Dad was the first to reach Mum, followed by Recco. Shoes, clothes and photo frames lay awkwardly amongst the scrubs that sat beneath the living-room windows.

Mum stood in her nightgown, unaware of the cold rain, screaming against the wind that tousled her hair and lifted the hem of her nightie.

'You've stolen my family!' she raged. 'Give me back my family!' Malice rang in her unshaking voice.

'Linda, calm down,' Dad managed.

The photo frame carved through the night air, narrowly missing Recco's cheek. The smiling faces of Shell and me lay bare on the damp grass.

'Stop, Linda!' Dad screamed, desperation and embarrassment ringing in his voice.

She screamed a long and haunting scream, drawing Shell and me to the open front door. Tears began to flow without hindrance or shame, and we shook, mortified, embarrassed and devastated all at once. Our crazy, twisted family life was now revealed; the entire road bore witness to the tortured lives we had been living for the past sixteen years.

'That's enough,' Dad shouted. 'Don't you dare throw another thing!'

Mum stood, glaring at Dad, legs rooted firmly. There was a terrible silence, and I felt my skin prickle. The ten-second standoff seemed to last a lifetime – one army stood facing the other, weapons at the ready. Mum was poised, fists clenched, while Dad was armed only with his drive to protect us. Slowly, the silent, prickling atmosphere began to morph into a feeling that we recognised, and the hairs on my neck hardened and bristled. The soldiers stood tall on their haunches, preparing to strike.

With the strength and agility of a deadly commando, Mum leapt, her feet sailing over the darkened ground, and with almost gentle grace, her arm swung into Dad's unprotected face. Dad buckled but did not fall, his breath held in stasis. Blood poured down his cheek.

'I think you had better leave now, Linda,' said Recco, his Italian accent making the suggestion sound almost friendly.

Mum's spent anger could not fuel her fight any longer. She retreated, broken triumph in her eyes, to her safe zone across the road. She didn't say a word, didn't look back at the children she'd left behind. Even after surviving yet another unprovoked attack, Dad would ensure that the triumphant but wounded soldier returned safely, would make sure she got to bed all right, ready to wake the following morning with no memory of the battle she'd fought the night before and the devastation she'd wrought.

8

GOLDFISH AT MY WINDOW

When your world is turned upside down, everything becomes unfamiliar. The usual morphs into something unrecognisable, alien and formidable. The most basic everyday tasks become a test; the habitual routine is redefined and redrawn. The accustomed route home is now a labyrinthine challenge, there to test you when you try to reach your old life. The changing colours of the front doors and buildings you pass are there to remind you of the adjustments your body and mind have had to make, and the alternating sounds and faces that you encounter paint even those closest to you in strange, terrifying shades.

If I were to tell you that the changes we faced delivered a new era of happiness and contentment, I would be lying. The promise of a new beginning was always a lie, for the baggage of mental illness never leaves. Mum was still at home fighting the same mental illness. We'd found no magical cure, reached no sudden realisations – the illness just changed shape, and the problems just moved. We could never walk away and leave it all behind. We felt a responsibility: an accountability for the woman we'd left behind. After her attack on Jill's house, Dad, Shell and I began checking in on Mum every day. The guilt that we felt propelled us to cook, clean and pay the bills. We dared hope for forgiveness, redemption even. Mum would sit and watch as we worked silently, both parties unprepared to say anything that might spark conflict.

Once, Dad went to visit alone but did not return. It had been hours since he should have been home, and no one was picking up Mum's phone. Finally, at around ten o'clock that evening, while Shell and I were blindly watching TV, Dad walked through the door with what looked like a turban on his head. We would have laughed but for the sorry look on his face.

'What happened? What did she do this time?' we asked in an almost nonchalant way.

Dad removed the white bandage to reveal the raw, red flesh of his scalp shining through his thick, dark hair.

'Boiling water from the kettle,' he said, 'and I didn't even get a cup of tea.' He gave us a weary half smile.

'Perhaps you need to wear a tin hat next time you go,' I said, trying to make light of the awful situation.

* * *

Finally, our new beginning began. The flat's peeling front door was accessed through a courtyard of overgrown weeds, broken fence panels and rubbish bins. A short flight of stairs led to our kitchen, which held an aging fridge and an oven with one working hob ring. The wooden floor sloped slightly, so if you were wearing socks and the floor was clean, you could slide towards the sink with just a gentle push. The living room was large, and the open fire and exposed oak beams gave the room the air of tradition and sophistication that, as a carpenter, Dad had longed for. There were three bedrooms, boasting nothing but peeling wallpaper and mouldy underlay, but we saw them as canvases to paint and dreams to mould. So Dad, being the selfless man that he was, took the smallest, dampest and most depressing room at the back, allowing Shell and me to choose between the two biggest and brightest rooms.

That first evening, we sat on the rolled-up carpet eating noodles, a musty smell drifting from the secondhand under-lay. Shell dropped a knot of tangled noodles on the floor, and sauce flipped up onto her cheek and into her eye. Both Dad and I turned to look, and with deep intakes of breath and sarcastic smiles, we returned to our gourmet meal. We had spent the day moving donated furniture, bedding and kitchenware into our new home, and we were exhausted. Every muscle sang with tired but happy weariness, and the relief that we felt outweighed the nagging fear of the future.

That night, the tiredness overcame the lumps in our mattresses and the scratchiness of the worn-out linen. All three of us slept deeply, knowing that the madness was a mile away. We hoped that the distance would protect us, would act as a deep and uncrossable divide that would save us from the disturbed nights we had become so accustomed to.

We spent the next few weeks painting, cleaning and adjusting to our new lives. It was a new and unfamiliar routine, and we warmed to it quickly. With each fresh coat of paint, we felt renewed. The pale-yellow eggshell that covered almost every wall in the flat glowed with promise, and our hope grew.

After a particularly strenuous Saturday of painting over cracked walls and chipped skirting boards, we sat eating spaghetti at the wooden picnic bench that now acted as our kitchen table. The slightly hard spaghetti covered in tomato sauce crunched uncomfortably between my teeth, and I could tell by the turned-up noses of my fellow diners that Dad and Shell were thinking the same. It didn't get any better; the fruitcake we had for dessert was covered with a thin, runny liquid that was apparently custard but had the texture and colour of fresh bird poo.

'I never know how to make custard properly,' I said, trying to explain myself.

'There is an easy way to test it,' Dad said as he spooned a portion of custard and threw it at the kitchen wall in front of us.

The custard immediately slithered down the wall and landed on the floor in a pool, leaving a questionable yellow streak down the otherwise-clean wall.

'Nope, it's not done,' he said, giving us that sideways smile that meant he knew he was being cheeky.

From that day on, that was the custard test. On

pudding nights, you would find us throwing custard at the newly painted kitchen wall – if it stuck and slithered gently down the wall, it was perfect; if it ran, we'd put it back on for a few more minutes. Then, under strict experimental conditions, another test sample would be hurled at the wall. Initial results did indicate that the shiny surface of the eggshell was not conducive to accurately demonstrating custard thickness, so the wall with a matt finish became the surface of choice.

On one such evening, the custard test had gone well the first time, and there'd been no need for a retest. We sat in silent contemplation, musing over the day's events, when Dad suddenly announced that he didn't like the newly applied egg yellow of the walls. He suggested that Shell and I should paint pictures directly onto the walls using the left-over Dulux paints donated by friends. That evening, Shell and I began our creations. My own masterpiece was a painted window drawn directly above the windowless sink and draining board. Through the window, goldfish with large cartoon eyes swam past, white bubbles escaping from their open mouths. Seaweed snaked up from the depths, partially obscured by a white frame. If you looked closely, you'd find a pair of big eyes peering from behind a clump of sea grass and a sunken treasure chest filled with pink and white pearls. From then on, whenever I was washing up dirty bowls of custard, I would imagine myself swimming with the goldfish. Bubbles of air followed my feet as I played hide-and-seek with them, and the blades of seaweed and sea grass swayed as I searched for the lost treasure.

On the opposite wall, a tall willow tree stood slightly crooked, as if it had been blown over in the wind. The leaves were an odd shade of lime green (Shell had been restricted by the selection of colours on offer), and at the base of the tree, Zoe, our eight-year-old Dalmatian, stood with one leg cocked. Bonnie, the Jack Russell, sat nearby, peering out from the wall.

The paintings remained on the walls until we left four years later. They served as a reminder that, even during the days of anguish and anxiety that were to follow, there could still be laughter. Whatever we were forced to face, we could find moments of lightness and relief just by glancing at the peeing dog or the goldfish hunting lost treasure.

* * *

Shell and I, now seventeen years old, had left school with reasonable grades. Shell achieved higher results so chose to stay on to do A levels, while I, in no uncertain terms, was told, 'I don't think A levels are for you, Lisa.' Instead, I chose to go to college for non-academic study: beauty therapy and hairdressing. I enjoyed my three years at the local college, but it did lead to me struggling once again with food. I felt that I was expected to look a certain way: thin and glamorous. I could easily achieve the thin, but being glamorous did not come easily, as my rampant acne was hard to hide, even under four feet of foundation. While my anorexia became louder and more insistent, Shell found it difficult to settle into sixth form. While she had one good friend, Shell became more and more isolated and began to struggle with the demands of three science A levels. It was difficult for Shell to escape the town that we were slaves to; as our school was nearby, she continued under the eyes of teachers and friends that had long been witnesses to our lives. In the end, Shell failed her exams, which only served to deepen her developing depression.

At a college located twenty-five miles away, I found it easy to slot into a well-rehearsed character that I could use to recreate and develop myself. I was no longer the anxiety-consumed, anorexic girl with a troubled life – I was the slightly underwhelming girl with high aspirations for a better (but still normal) life. I played my new character well and made friends quickly. My skinny frame and makeup-covered face hid the real me, and I led my second life with a ruby-red smile.

* * *

The meagre money that Dad brought home every week was stretched to the breaking point by the demands of running two households. With the addition of the money Shell and I brought home from our Saturday shifts at Tesco, we were able to fill the flat with a sofa that would look more at home in the floral, carpeted home of an eighty-year-old. It sat awkwardly alongside the polished-copper bombshell casings from Dad's personal collection of Second World War memorabilia.

We had been in our new home for around three months

before we found the courage to invite Mum over for dinner. Finally, the ever-grinding guilt of leaving her behind drove us to extend the arm of forgiveness and compassion that Mum would not. She perched on the worn brown sofa with her back stiff, her face a mask of unease and suspicion. The atmosphere was uncomfortable, the silence punctuated by bursts of lame and unnatural conversation. Mum and Dad seemed like strangers making polite conversation to pass the time at a bus stop. Laughter was forced when Dad made jokes about my bad cooking, and Mum smiled like a cobra about to strike.

She surveyed her surroundings with trepidation, not knowing if the life that we had presented for her inspection was a life we were planning to remain in or not. The stranger never made comments or passed judgment, deigning instead to sit on our sofa rarely speaking. On occasion, she acknowledged our poor attempts at humour with a smile that showed neither comprehension or emotion. Only her narrowed hazel eyes betrayed her true feelings. Dinner was swift, the roast potatoes and roast chicken consumed in an almost static silence, and Mum departed within minutes of the meal finishing, leaving Shell and me to quietly clear the table.

Dad returned, his pace heavy, uncertainty written on his face. When he saw us, his face contorted into a stiff smile. Shell and I sat on the edge of the sofa, pretending to watch the Sunday afternoon film – something about children being mistakenly shrunk to the size of bread crumbs.

'Dad, is everything okay?' Shell said, standing to hug him.

'Everything is fine. Don't worry, you doughnuts!'

The atmosphere relaxed, and warmth returned to the room as we treated ourselves to ice cream and the TV. As the children returned to their original size and were reunited with their worried but grateful parents, the phone began to ring. Dad picked up the handset and answered with his usual 'Bonjour'.

'Bonjour?' he repeated. 'Hello,' he said again, just in case the caller wasn't French. After a moment, he hung up. 'There's no one there,' he said, looking at our faces.

We were grinning madly. 'That's because it's the TV remote, Dad!'

As Dad answered the real phone, our laughter stopped with a sudden crash.

'Calm down, Lynn, we didn't—no, we weren't—Lynn, listen to—'

Shell and I were immediately on the defensive, backs stiff and hearts thumping.

Dad looked at us and rolled his eyes in an attempt to lighten the mood. It wasn't working. My mouth was dry, and I could feel the blood being pulled from my face.

'Why would we make fun of you?' he continued, all playfulness now forgotten.

We could hear Mum's screams echoing down the phone line.

Dad returned the phone to the coffee table without even a goodbye.

'She put the phone down,' he said. After a moment, he smiled weakly. 'Don't worry, you know the routine. She will put herself to bed for a couple of days, and it will be back to normal.' He may as well have been telling us that Mum wasn't really ill and that she was about to jump out from behind the door and say, 'Surprise, I am not really mad!'

* * *

I am naked again, but this time I am standing on the grassy roundabout at the bottom of our road. A car slows as it enters the left lane. The driver stares at my white flesh as the car veers off route. I panic and try to lurch towards a nearby hedge, hoping to find something to cover myself with. My body doesn't move; my legs are heavy, and my feet remain still, my body toppling to the ground, revealing a rare midday full moon. The now-stationary car honks its horn.

I lie on the ground, everything moving in slow motion. As I try desperately to drag myself towards the camouflage of the foliage, I hear a phone ringing. Wait – phones on roundabouts? Since when? The ringing becomes louder, but I can't see the source anywhere. As the roundabout begins to fade beneath a thick white mist and the grass sinks away into the soft, undulating mounds of my mattress, my eyes begin to blink.

The bedroom was in darkness. The luminous orange characters of my digital clock told me it was 11:35 p.m. The ringing had stopped, but had been replaced by the sound of Dad's hushed but urgent voice. I found him already in the living room, talking quietly to Shell. The phone sat silent and peaceful on the coffee table.

'Was that Mum again?' I asked, already knowing the answer.

'It's all right, love, go back to bed.' He turned to Shell. 'You too, Shell. You both have school tomorrow.'

'No, Dad, what's happening?' Shell asked, anxiety in her eyes.

'Your Mum's just having one of those days. Remember, she is all the way over on the other side of town, and it's late. She can't get to us.'

Even at seventeen, Shell and I were comforted by the huge, enveloping arms of Dad. He would squeeze so hard that it was difficult to breathe, and we'd have to suck in deep breaths of air when we finally surfaced from his thick, woolly jumper.

* * *

I can feel my fingertips burning. My nails dig into the loose gravel, and my feet scramble at the soft rock, searching desperately for purchase. The ache shoots through my arms and into my shoulders, and my muscles scream for me to let go. I look down at the angry waves crashing against the base of the cliff, and I feel their force shake the rock beneath my fingers. The sky is dark, and as the lightning crackles above, I feel the thunder shake the world. I grip even tighter. Small rocks and clouds of dust rain down upon me, and I slam my eyes shut, trembling on the rock face, the thunder ringing in my ears. I wonder if this is the time that I'll lose my grip and fall into the hungry waves below.

Another thunderous crash, but this time from below. As I crane my eyes to the dark waters, the earth begins to open. Bright light breaks through the ravine, which is fast carving a wide canyon below me. I blink, tears falling from my eyes – it's so bright now I can barely see. I hear Dad shouting something. Is he here to save me? If he is, why is he screaming Mum's name?

* * *

I awoke to light streaming through the gap of my open door. I looked at my clock – 2:16 a.m. The screaming was becoming angry, and thunder seemed to tremble down the hallway. I left the safety of my room behind and joined Shell in the narrow hall. She stood outside Dad's bedroom door, frozen to the frayed cream carpet, stuck in a scene that spun and teased and frothed.

Mum's left hand was buried in Dad's scalp. She dragged him from his bed, and blood began to slide from the puncture wounds above his forehead and gather in his greying eyebrows. Mum was still wearing the blue-flowered dress that she'd worn to dinner eight hours earlier, but her black slip-on shoes had been replaced by brown sheepskin slippers. Her skin was pale, her lips tight, and her cheeks moved in and out with every manic breath.

'Lynn,' Dad shouted, 'stop!'

Mum's only reply was to scream wordlessly.

'Mum, please stop!' we begged through desperate and broken sobs.

I fell to my knees, the cries leaving me in such a hurry I could hardly breathe. It almost felt as though my heart was crying, its tears flooding my lungs. Shell joined the chorus of screams, but no one seemed to hear.

With a sudden surge of fury, Dad gripped Mum's left wrist and pulled her hand from his head, black hair thick between her fingers. Mum's eyes shot wide, and a tremor shook her. As she realised she was losing the battle, a small knife held almost unseen in her right hand appeared above Dad's head, hovering like an angry wasp.

The silence sucked the oxygen from the room, and for a moment, our breath hovered just millimetres from our starving bodies. As the knife began its journey down, I felt the ripples of moving air in its wake and felt my skin split. The blade sank into Dad's shoulder, and he cried out, shrinking away from the pain. Mum pulled her hand away as if she'd been struck, and the knife remained, protruding from Dad's flesh, the wooden handle wobbling as he moved.

Blood began to trace the contours of Dad's muscular back. Calmly, Dad gripped the wooden handle and pulled the blade from its resting place, showing no signs of pain or injury. He stood, his six-foot frame towering defiantly over Mum, who seemed suddenly weak and miniscule. Her eyelids fluttered, and at once she began screaming again. She fell against the wall with arms outstretched, reaching for a redemption that would never come.

Still Shell and I remained stationary, muscles taut, bodies still. Every cell in my brain screamed at me to move, but the terror was too strong.

Exhausted and spent, Mum sat with her back against the wall, her legs splayed out before her. Her shoulders quivered as her sobs slowed, and her eyes remained fixed on her hands, which shook uncontrollably. Blood dried beneath her fingernails, but still she did not see the devastation she had caused – only the victim she believed she was.

Without emotion, Dad pulled Mum from her self-pity and, with almost aggressive force, moved Mum down the narrow, winding stairs to the kitchen.

'Get out!' we heard him scream.

'Bastard,' came Mum's reply. The door slammed. 'Bastards!' she continued to scream as she stumbled through the darkened courtyard and out onto the empty road.

Shell and I ran down the stairs, narrowly avoiding each other's flapping arms and legs. Dad must have suddenly become aware of the wound in his shoulder, for we found him sitting on the kitchen bench, trying in vain to examine the gaping hole. The wound was deep this time, but still we had to bribe Dad into going to hospital.

Shell and I sat blindly staring at the TV as we waited for Dad to return. One of his conditions had been that we both had to go back to bed while he went to the hospital alone. Of course, sleep evaded us – our minds were locked in the hallway, the same five minutes on continual replay. As the blue neon lights of the TV blinked in the corner of the living room, I peered through the window at the main road below, waiting for the white Ford van to pull off the street into the narrow drive.

Every two minutes I would turn to the kitchen door, expecting Dad to emerge from its now-broken frame. Mum in her rage had managed to force the front door open, breaking the lock on the internal door. The splinters of the white wood remained on the floor, a reminder of the violence that had been forced upon it.

Dad had been gone for over two hours. Eyes wide, I peered through the darkness at the church across the road. The first pale wisps of sunlight were struggling to break the night, granting the horizon a murky orange blush. There, beneath the church, a lone figure moved without direction or purpose through the graveyard. I strained my eyes, but in my heart I knew it was Dad.

I traced the thick lines of the goldfish's cartoon eyes with my finger, my eyes glazed. In my head, the sad, lonely figure walked on amongst the graves, looking for something he'd never find. I wondered what he'd been thinking about, whether he'd been mulling over the night's events, trying to vent his anger, or, worse, had simply not wanted to come home. After all, coming home would have meant questions to which he had no answers and two terrified girls he felt he could not comfort. The illusion we'd shared that the flat was our fortress, our protection, was gone.

9

WHEN RUSHING RIVERS DIVIDE

The thin yellow material swished around my ankles as I swayed my hips back and forth, trying to keep pace with the slow rhythm of 'The Time of My Life' from *Dirty Dancing*. I couldn't remember the name of the boy who'd asked me to dance; I wasn't even sure what he looked like, as I'd spent the past two minutes staring at his feet, my arms fixed straight in front of me while he struggled to pull me closer. When the final notes rang out, I turned and ran, leaving the hall without even acknowledging the boy I'd been slow dancing with. The cold night air chilled my bare legs as I sped home in my new strappy sandals. Slowly, the tension that had been building in my body began to ease, and I started to cry. I felt an idiot. Why couldn't I be like everyone else? It should have been so easy for me, a seventeen-year-old, to enjoy the attention of boys, but I felt sick. Feeling his hands on my bony ribs and his breath whistling past my ear had made my skin crawl and my mind convulse and run.

I felt like a weirdo, a strange oddity who didn't deserve the attentions of others. Why, I thought, would anyone want to look at me? I was fat and ugly and couldn't bring happiness to anyone, so why should I even dream of it?

That night was one of disturbed, fitful sleep. I dreamed of yellow dresses, hot breath and lies. The next day, I leaned against the fixed kitchen door (after Mum's attack, Dad had screwed the kitchen door to the frame for the sake of security) and told Dad how I'd danced to Duran Duran and been chatted up by a plethora of boys. It was the story of a normal teenage girl doing normal teenage things, and it seemed to placate Dad's anxiety and give him faith in the idea that our lives could run along normally.

The sun streamed through the bare windows of my bedroom, painting my world red through my eyelids. It was Sunday morning, and the church bells rang the call for morning service. I pulled the duvet over my head. My belief that God was looking out for us had long passed, and I wasn't about to get out of bed to say thanks. I simply couldn't believe in an omnipotent and supremely benevolent being who still allowed so much torment.

The day was bright and dry, and I realised I couldn't stay in bed forever. That afternoon, we decided to walk along the river a few miles from where we lived. After removing the security screws once more, we were met by a perplexing and worrying sight. Just outside the front door, in the shadows of the overhanging weeds, stood Brambles Coffee Shop's sign, gently swinging from its hinges in the breeze. Alongside it stood a red fire extinguisher and a plant pot with the words *Welcome to Halstead, Winner of Town in Bloom Award 1987* printed in thick black letters on the side.

We stood for what felt like an hour trying to figure out the puzzle that lay broken before us. When the pieces finally fell into place, we saw only the face of Mum laughing at us. Why had Mum dragged these things from the town centre all the way out here? What was she trying to tell us? Was it some deranged attempt to lead the police to our door?

We spent the next hour returning the stolen items to their rightful owners. Being unaware of where the fire extinguisher originated, we left it outside Brambles, hoping it and the sign had come as a pair. Thankfully, the town was in its usual soulless, empty state, and we were able to go about our work unnoticed. It appeared that we had gotten away scot-free from our brush with the law, so we celebrated with 'fancy' ice cream from Tesco, a video rented from Blockbuster and a brand new five-lever mortise lock from a budget DIY warehouse.

* * *

We spent each evening for the next week on high alert, anticipating a phone call or a bang at the door, but it never came. Shell and I would return from our respective schools to find Dad asleep on the old velour sofa with a glass of Bacardi and Coke held precariously, the clear liquid about to spill into his lap. This was becoming an increasingly common sight. He insisted that he'd only have a couple of drinks 'to relax his old bones'. Over the next few years, we would start finding empty Bacardi and other rum bottles hidden in bins, under piles of clothes and underneath his bed. At the time, Dad's descent into alcoholism went unnoticed. He wore a mask of happiness and control, which threw people off the scent of his self-destruction. As the alcohol softened his inhibitions, Dad found it easier and easier to play the loveable fool – it was only when he returned to his bed that he was alone. Alcohol became his friend, and it was the only thing that brought relief from whatever terrified him in his dreams.

When addiction bites, it holds on tight. It glues itself to its victim, and I watched as it began to strangle Dad, dictating his actions with its ever-demanding need. I grieved for the loss that Dad must have felt, and I imagined the cycle that was spinning out of control in his mind, for I had been – and was still – in the grip of my own addiction to anorexia. I often wonder if it was happiness or redemption that the alcohol offered. Perhaps it gave Dad moments of happy forgetfulness, respite from the challenges that the everyday dramas brought.

On the good days, Dad appeared as his old self: a joker with the kindest heart you could imagine and the hug of a titan. But I knew that for all his outer strength, Dad was a man who lacked the durability needed to live the life that had been forged for him. Always believing that the world was eventually going to deliver happiness and relief, he possessed the common sense and naïve hope of a five-year-old. There were times when we had to restrict the weekly grocery shop to the bare minimum as he had 'forgotten' to pay his taxes. We lived for a while eating beans on toast and tins of macaroni cheese while every spare penny went to the taxman or Mum. On one occasion, charged with babysitting a goldfish, he panicked when he returned home to see it floating in its bowl, which sat on a sunny windowsill. Dad thought he could revive the fish with a quick cooldown in the freezer. Unfortunately for the fish, Dad fell asleep. Apparently, it's not a good idea to return a goldfish lollipop to an eight-year-old child.

On the bad days, he retreated into his quiet and lonely world. There were no words or smiles – only a pale, defeated face that hung above a glass of Bacardi, staring blindly into a world that was denying him the happiness and relief he'd long hoped for. On these days, I suspected he was slowly accepting that the time was up – he'd been left with nothing more than a rented flat and van that he would never own. The only certainty that remained and endured was the love he felt for his girls. He would instil in Shell and me the belief that we could be whatever we wanted and achieve whatever we wished to. Our floundering and wilting confidence were lifted by Dad's total belief in us. He knew we'd craft better lives for ourselves than the one he'd been given.

* * *

When the rains arrive, torrents of water flood the rivers. The swelling tide pushes and grinds at the banks and, as the pressure grows, the water breaks the confines of the river-banks and cascades, breaking from the course that has been preordained. The new path diverts around tree roots and rocks to discover new lands and new beginnings. This new, young stream has a picture and personality of its own. It may survive the test of time, or it may end as a memory that lacked the strength and force of its ancestor and now lies dry and long-forgotten.

Shell and I were desperately pushing at our own confining banks in a frenzied attempt to avoid the path that Mum had been forced down. We had secretly made a pact that we were not going to live our lives as Mum had; we would do all that we could to avert the predetermined path that genetics had drawn for us. We went so far as to promise to shoot each other if we showed signs of turning into Mother. Mum often said that we had delusions of grandiosity, but all we wanted were normal lives with normal opportunities. We never wanted to be superstars with boats and gold-covered helicopters.

At the age of twenty-one, both Shell and I started to forge our own rivers. My own trickling stream had joined another forceful flow, and I married Darryl. Just a few days after the wedding, I left the safety of the main river and moved to North Yorkshire, joining the Royal Air Force as a forces wife. Meanwhile, Shell enlisted in the RAF to train as an aeronautical engineer. Our rivers had divided: mine meandered and mingled with the other small, weak streams, trying to find a strong current to embrace, while Shell's raged and roared, its own current building as it went. Both our rivers had originated from the same turbulent source, and both sought the same calm, clear water, the same glittering oasis.

The door opened to reveal the smiling face of Shell. We hugged each other for what seemed like an age.

'Ooh I've missed you, sis,' I said as I pulled away. I looked into her eyes, and something was wrong, but I couldn't see it.

'Why are you looking at me like that?' Shell asked as her brow furrowed tightly. I paused, unsure of what to say. 'Nothing, I've just missed you,' I lied. She grinned and pulled me in for another hug.

I sat cross-legged on her bed, and Shell sat close to me, leaning her back against the wall. My spirit lifted with happiness as we talked and laughed, seemingly without stopping for breath. I looked around the cramped RAF quarters, and I saw family photos and Shell's pencil drawings stuck to the wall, which gave the room a familiar feeling. The two months of tough basic training was evident in her slim, toned body and tired eyes. The young, shy and slightly pudgy girl that had left three months ago had found another stream to follow.

We paused for a moment from the constant laughing, and Shell asked, 'How are things with Mum?'

'Umm . . .' I replied, raising my eyebrows with warning.

'That bad!' she said with a huff.

'It's hard,' I said, unable to tell her the truth.

Shell looked down at her lap and began to fiddle with the hem of her shirt. 'I am sorry, Lee.'

'It's not your fault; you're a hundred miles away. You can't just pop round when it gets bad.' I held back the words that were pressing on my tongue.

'I feel bad that you have to deal with it all.'

I playfully pushed her shoulder to snap her out of her dull mood. 'You could actually phone her now and again,' I said as I waved my finger in jest. 'It takes the heat off me for a day or two.' My playfulness failed to lift her.

'I know, but I can't cope with it now.' Shell avoided my eyes and continued to pull at a loose thread.

I didn't say anything for a moment. I contemplated whether I should continue the conversation, but instead I jumped off the bed. 'Come on, let's get drunk.'

Shell looked at me, and a mischievous grin appeared. 'First round on you then.'

I emptied the last drops of Merlot into my glass, and I felt the fuzzy warmth that it gave me. Shell spurted out a guffaw of laughter. 'You will never guess what Dad did the other day.' She finished her drink before continuing. 'I was on the phone to him when he started making noises like he was having a heart attack or something.'

'What?' I said with genuine concern.

'He had glued his glasses to his eyebrows and was trying to pull them off.' We both exploded in a fit of laughter, and the diners at the next table turned to show their disapproval.

'Why were they glued to his eyebrows?' I said, still laughing.

'They had snapped in the middle, and because he

couldn't see without them he was gluing them while he was wearing them.' Another spurt of laughter caused more disapproving looks from next door.

'I am so full,' Shell said as she leaned back in her chair and rubbed her flat belly. 'But I think I could manage some dessert. What do you reckon?'

After licking the last of the ice cream from her spoon, Shell sat quietly in her chair. 'You okay?' I asked. Her eyes narrowed, and her face became pale.

'Yeah, I am just popping to the loo,' she replied without looking at me.

Shell was gone for what felt like ages, so I decided to visit the loo myself before heading back. I opened the bathroom door to find Shell at the sink. She leaned on the countertop, her eyes cast down, gazing at her hands. 'Shell?' I said with anxiety. She didn't respond. 'Shell!' I said louder as I gripped her arm. She spun round as if I had woken her from a nightmare. I stepped back, frightened by what I saw. Shell stared at me with wide, scared eyes. Her face was deathly pale, which exaggerated the black circles that surrounded her red, watery eyes. Her hands started to shake as tears formed. The familiar feeling of fear started to hammer against my nerves.

'Shell, what is it?' My voice shook with panic.

'I am sorry, Lee. I can't help it.' She paused and breathed deeply. 'It makes me feel better if I bring it all back up.'

'Shell, please tell me you're not making yourself sick?'

Shell remained silent, and her gaze returned to her

hands. The door to the bathroom opened with a bang, and a lady looked at us with suspicion as she entered a cubicle. 'Let's get out of here,' Shell said as she rubbed her eyes with shaky hands.

Back in her room we sat without speaking. I now understood the unease I felt when I first arrived. I also understood Shell's reasons for punishing her body in this way. The desire for control had trapped Shell too.

WHEN DRAGONS FLY

The dragon had flown. Its large, powerful wings opened, and it soared. The currents lifted the powerful beast, and he flew above the earth, high above the pain and torment that had kept him earthbound. There was no pain to drag him down. His eyes were open, and he soared into the horizon to find peace where the other dragons flew.

'Let's have another cup of tea,' I said, smiling at Mum, who sat on the old green-leather sofa.

She said nothing but looked up at me, the cigarette about to burn her fingers.

'I'll find some biscuits.' I moved the ashtray under the burning cigarette.

'I don't have any biscuits,' Mum suddenly said. 'I haven't eaten for weeks; I don't have any food. I might as well die now.'

I rolled my eyes.

As I boiled the kettle, I found an unopened packet of custard creams behind the tins of beans, soup and mushy peas. There were no clean mugs left in the cupboard, so I spent ten minutes clearing the mountain of dirty dishes in the sink. I looked out onto the overgrown grass of the back garden, and all at once tormented memories flickered through my mind.

'Lee.' Mum's voice broke my reverie. 'Lee, what are you doing?' There was a pause. 'I think I need some of those lead lights for the garden.'

'Lead lights? What do you mean?'

'Lead lights – you know, the ones you put in the ground that use the sun.'

'Do you mean solar?'

'Yeah, but aren't they called lead lights?'

'Do you mean LED?' I said, trying not to laugh.

'Yeah, LED. Does it mean London Electricity Department?'

I nodded, smirking. It was easier to agree. 'Yes Mum, London Electricity Department!'

The laugh that I was stifling escaped in a burst of air, and my tea spilled on my hand.

It's funny how a cup of tea can change so much. A mug of hot, milky tea and a custard cream banished Mum's death wish and instead had her contemplating the 'London Electricity Department' and garden lighting. My anxiety melted away as Mum laughed with me. For a moment, a flicker of love softened my mother – but something glued me to my seat, preventing me from rushing to her and holding her tight.

* * *

It was 2001. After ten years, I was back in Essex with Darryl, Hayley (my six-year-old daughter) and Bonnie the Jack Russell. We lived in a three-bedroom semi that we couldn't really afford, and I'd just been awarded my Bachelor of Science degree in diagnostic radiography. I secretly yearned to confront the teacher at school who had told me I was too thick for A levels and to delicately place my rolled-up degree where the sun don't shine.

We lived just a few miles away from the oak-beamed, ivy-covered cottage Shell owned. Dad lived there now, being unable to afford a home of his own, and though he was reliant on his children financially, we were still reliant on him for support and comfort. We'd long since left the flat behind, and our separate streams had merged again, re-forming the rushing river that had divided years ago. It felt good to be close again. So many things had changed for Shell and me, but nothing had moved forwards in the backstreets of Mum and Dad's relationship. Without his guardians present, Dad's dependence on alcohol had begun to dominate. As with all dependencies, it soon reached past Dad, extending its influence to the people around him. Shell and I now faced the pressures of both madness and alcoholism – not to mention the added side order of our own eating disorders.

Although Shell had left the RAF after seven years, she was still away from home for weeks on end, installing commercial radar around the world. This was how she met her now-husband – in the Arctic Circle, of all places! I admit to grinning with pride when I speak of the sheer bloody-mindedness of Shell and me. To be honest, the only reason that Shell and I hadn't given in to the easy and demanding pull of depression was the solid and immovable love and support of Dad.

Once, the only doctor in the surgery who would deal with Mum recognised me. 'I can't believe how . . . *normal* you and your sister have turned out,' he said.

I think it was a compliment, but it did demonstrate what the world had predicted for me and Shell, and I felt proud that we had blown that predetermined path to smithereens.

Of course, every miraculous path has a slab of concrete at its end, determined to derail your journey and catch every foot that tries to pass. Shell and I are facing that concrete, sledgehammers and pickaxes in hand.

* * *

Hayley squealed in horrified delight as Dad threw her into the air.

'Grandad! Stop!' she laughed. 'No, no Grandad!'

I watched with my eyes half closed and my teeth clenched. Hayley's head had just missed the oak beam above.

'Who wants a Kit Kat?' Dad sang, returning Hayley to the ground to my great relief.

'Me!' Hayley shouted.

Dad hobbled off to the kitchen. I noticed him wince.

'What have you done to your leg?' I asked, following him into the kitchen, surreptitiously making sure that he wasn't secretly planning on filling Hayley with yet more sugar-filled treats.

'The doctor says I have a bit of gout in my foot, and it's playing me up a bit,' he said, pouring himself another glass of Bacardi and Coke.

'Well, you know what you need to do to stop it flaring up, don't you?' I nodded accusingly at the glass he held in his hand.

'Oh come on, it's Easter. Jesus drank wine, didn't he?' He grinned suddenly. 'And I am a carpenter, after all. I'm pretty much halfway to being ordained!'

I took a deep breath and rolled my eyes, returning my gaze to his foot. 'Let me have a look.' I noticed Hayley in the corner of the kitchen, about to tuck into a five-pack of Kit Kats.

He removed his shoe and sock and pulled up the leg of his baggy jeans. His foot was swollen and red up to his calf, and the skin appeared shiny and waxy.

'I'm no doctor, but that doesn't look like gout to me, Dad. I think you need to go back and get that checked out.'

'Yes, Doctor,' he said with a salute.

I laughed, and we returned to the happy day, not sparing another thought for the clot forming in Dad's leg.

* * *

The next day was Easter Sunday. After I'd run an egg hunt in the back garden and had a defeated conversation with Hayley as to why she wasn't allowed to eat eight Easter eggs at once, Dad arrived for a roast-chicken dinner. He limped into the kitchen, already out of breath.

'What the hell, Dad?'

He sat heavily on the sofa, and I put his leg up on the coffee table. I struggled to slide his jeans up over his enlarged calf. The whole lower leg shone a deep purple hue. When I brushed my hand over the engorged flesh, Dad expelled a huff of pain, his entire body stiffening.

'Right, that's it,' I said as I picked up the phone. 'Sorry everyone, dinner's off. We are seeing the emergency doctor in half an hour.'

Dad groaned like a child being told to have a bath before bed, but he didn't resist. I could see the pain in his eyes, which he was trying to hide.

* * *

I would do anything to change that day. If I spun around fast enough, could I reverse time like Superman did? If I stopped the sun from setting and the moon from rising, could I change the future? Could I freeze everyone in the time before, stopping the clock from catching up with us? If I promised to give my organic body back to the earth and my soul back to God, would he change his mind? Would he let Dad stay?

* * *

One table, one rug, three . . . no, four chairs and a vase. Were those real sunflowers in the vase, or fake? No matter how long I looked, I couldn't seem to *see* them. They might not have been there at all. Maybe I was not really there. Could I really trust what I saw in front of me? Perhaps this was all a nightmare. Just as the sunflower stems seemed to magically bend where they entered the water, just as my irises grew and shrank depending on the light, it could all have been an illusion. How could I trust the images before me? In a dream, the picture constantly changes, the faces often blank. Objects and landscapes move in and out of focus, the edges hazy and indistinguishable.

This was the worst day of my life: the day Dad woke up.

* * *

'I am sorry,' the doctor said, 'but there is nothing we can do for your dad. We will do everything we can to make him comfortable.'

I was sitting in my manager's office at work. A very nice, soft-spoken doctor was explaining to me that Dad was going to die.

I stare at him without a word. He must have thought I

didn't hear him, for he repeated himself without even mentioning the word 'cancer'.

'The blood clot that travelled from your dad's leg to his lungs has been treated, but I am afraid that he is not strong enough to cope with any of the remaining treatments we can offer.'

The blood drained from my body. I didn't hear anything else the doctor said – all I could think was, *Why is the doctor afraid?* Shouldn't that be Dad's job? Or mine? After all, I was the one who'd have to tell Shell that Dad wouldn't be here to keep us safe, to give us the love that we so desperately needed.

* * *

I asked God, *Are we here only to be taken away when You will it?*

If God does exist and He created humans, then we must have a purpose; so why take us before we have fulfilled that purpose? Why give us the pain of loss? Can this omniscient, all-knowing being explain to me *why*? Why take the good and leave the bad? Religion would say that we must not fear death, for our souls will be loved and cared for, but it was not Dad's death I feared. I feared the *process* of him dying, the pain he would suffer and the loss that we would feel after he was gone. It was the prospect of a life without Dad that most terrified me.

I asked God for a miracle, but he must have been busy that day.

* * *

The weak figure lay in the makeshift bedroom that had once been our dining room. He was talking to his brother, Peter, who'd died two years previously. He told him that he'd be seeing him soon. I wondered if it was the morphine talking or whether he really could see his brother – was he sending his RSVP to God's party? I looked at the empty space where Uncle Peter must have been standing, and I imagined him smiling, telling Dad that everything was going to be okay and that it wasn't so bad in heaven. I smiled, the tears diverting around the corners of my mouth. I wiped them away with the back of my hand and returned to the dinner I was cooking.

For the next week, I slept on a mattress outside the dining-room door and spent my days emptying blood-filled commodes. Dad slipped in and out of reality, and in moments of confusion he became angry. I didn't want him to know that the cancer was slowly stealing the person he used to be. When the angry stranger arrived, I would step in to stop him hurting himself or throwing his drinking glass at the door. He wept on my shoulder, telling me how scared he was, and all I could do was hug him. I had no words to comfort him, no answers to bring relief.

* * *

Dad spent his last days in the hospice. Shell and I never left his side. For eight days and nights we held his hand in the hope that he would feel our presence. He was heavily sedated – the pain the cancer caused was too much for any man to bear. We slept with our heads on his chest and our arms draped at his side, soaking in every last movement of his chest and every last echo of his breath. We ate and washed in a hurry for fear of missing his one last intake of air.

The autumn sun shone through the large windows by his bed, highlighting the motes of dust that danced in the air. I took a moment to watch them drift into a gentle blush of air that blew them suddenly aside and out of sight. I turned then to the other patients in the room and the other families keeping constant vigil. We would often smile at one another, dread and fear hidden deep behind our eyes. Although the polite and forced happy chatter rumbled, the pain of death hung in the air and sat heavily upon us. I returned my gaze to the movement of Dad's chest, the rise and fall bringing comfort and calm to the anxious beats of my heart.

On the eighth day, Dad woke up. His eyes opened, and his sparkling-blue gaze fell upon us. It was if he had just woken from a Sunday-afternoon nap on the sofa, after a heavy meal of roast beef and potatoes. He looked not like a man about to die, but one full of happy confusion. For a moment, I could believe that this was all a mistake and that the doctors had all gotten it wrong. He was my big, strong dad again, not the weak shadow that had taken his place. In those few moments, I realised that he didn't know that he was dying, that it was cancer that was eating him alive, and for that I am grateful.

He looked at us for what seemed like an age. He seemed to be studying every part of our faces, taking in every curve, every eyelash, every line of our trembling smiles.

'Hello,' he said.

Hello, Dad.

He closed his eyes again and died. He was fifty-five.

11

HELLO . . . IS THERE ANYBODY OUT THERE?

I was back on the slightly dirty cream carpet. I was breathing gently. Hayley stood over me.

'Mum, when is dinner?'

I smiled as I lifted my head, aware that my hair was still stuck to my tear-stained face.

'Chicken dinosaurs and smiley faces, okay?' I said.

'Yay!' Hayley exclaimed as she skipped from the room.

I rubbed my face roughly with my hands, trying to bring life back to my eyes and mind. I wiped away my tear-soaked hair and took a deep breath.

'Come on, Lisa, get a grip,' I said out loud. 'It's not all about you; get up off the floor, you pathetic woman!'

I pushed images of the Grim Reaper from my head and tried to focus. I couldn't remember how I had ended up on the floor with these unnatural thoughts in my mind. Images of Mum flashed in front of my eyes, and I saw myself as a child, looking upon her helpless face as she struggled against her own death wish. I remembered the feelings that my ten-year-old self struggled to comprehend, and tears bubbled to the surface once again. What was I doing? Would genetics win over human control after all? I told myself that it didn't have to be this way, that I didn't have to let depression win. I would dig my own path and lay its foundations deep and strong. Hayley would grow up without having to face the mountains and rivers that I was forced to overcome.

I spoke to God again as if He had just entered the room and sat down beside me.

'They say that You love me,' I said to the empty space in front of me.

'Of course, I love all my children,' God replied.

'Then why do You continue to punish me? Have I not said sorry a thousand times?'

God smiled at me. 'Did my Son not sacrifice Himself for your sins, Lisa? Your sins were nailed to the cross so that they may be forgiven.'

'Then why continue to punish me? Why take my dad from me? Why make Mum the way she is?'

'I do not punish, Lisa; I merely act on the sins that require discipline.'

'I don't understand! How is any of this *discipline*?'

'Through divine discipline, your eyes will open to what is good, Lisa, to what I have ordained for my children. Do you not discipline Hayley when she has done something wrong? Do you want her to learn what is right and what is wrong?'

'I asked for forgiveness because I don't love my husband

anymore. Is the guilt and depression not enough punishment? Have I not learnt my lesson?'

'No discipline is enjoyable, but what you will reap is a harvest of goodness and cleanliness.' God looked at me with a smile that radiated through me.

'But what did I do to deserve the pain of losing Dad? Why didn't You just hurt me and leave Dad here with us? Why?' I looked at His face with tears and anger in my eyes.

'I am Love, Lisa. Have faith, and you will find the answers you are looking for.'

God stood and left the room, leaving me with questions hanging in the air and depression in my heart. Even God had left me.

* * *

It was only two weeks after I'd lost Dad, the backbone to my life, when my husband began urgently talking about his needs. It had been difficult for him to adjust to the more confident and motivated wife who had emerged with a degree and a successful job, and I was unwilling to regress to the girl he'd married. I was in mourning, and my depression was deeper than it had ever been. My selfish needs only allowed me to care for Hayley, and the little that remained was just enough to keep me from the depths of the abyss, so Darryl's need to have me close felt both suffocating and unwanted.

By Christmas, I had moved out and was living in the cottage with Shell. My guilt was heavy, and I could not drag myself from the depression that was consuming me. I felt that everything I said and did was wicked, and I was sure I didn't deserve happiness. Again, my weight plummeted until my jeans could not grip the skinny frame they covered. It was Hayley who kept me alive. She was the sole reason I woke every day, and she alone filled me with the motivation to function as a human being. I returned to work after three months of caring for Dad, and with the help of some very special friends and the ever-damp shoulder of Shell, I crossed the starting line and began the race once more.

This time, it was a very lonely race. Without Dad holding my hand, the track became mountainous, with many sharp bends that tricked my eye and sent me sprawling in the dirt. Hayley and Shell were waiting at the finish line, but they were so far in the distance that I couldn't see them clearly.

It took three years for me to reach the finish, but by then my weight was stable and I believed in myself again. I had risen above the dark days, and I felt defiant.

* * *

After the divorce, I was left with a mirror, a chest of drawers and a small amount of cash. I walked away from the life I'd had, leaving the house and the majority of my possessions to Darryl. I fought only for Hayley. I couldn't allow her to live the life that I had.

With some financial help from my uncle, I bought a

two-bedroom terraced house not far from Shell's cottage and the hospice where Dad had spent his last days. I was overwhelmed by uncertainty, but the excitement of living in my own castle on my own terms had made my future seem like something worth fighting for.

While the paperwork was being completed, I continued to live with Shell in the cottage. Shell was often away in foreign lands or in Canada visiting Russ, which gave Hayley and me the entire cottage to ourselves. I continued to hide the darkness that would consume me alone at night so that Hayley would only experience the happy, strong mum that she deserved. We would spend the weekends baking cupcakes, roller skating and dancing to Disney songs as I strived to fill every second with happy memories, never allowing the torment that wrapped itself around my every nerve to be seen. I lived those first few months floating in the clouds, never knowing what each day would bring or whether an incorrect choice would bring about the end of the world.

On the first anniversary of Dad's death, Shell left me. She emigrated to Canada to be with Russ. She had found another family to be part of. I can never be angry or accuse her of abandoning me, as the comfort I gained from knowing that Shell had found happiness was vast and over-whelming. She had found deliverance, a path without sharp edges or ravines, and she had crossed her finish line without cuts or grazes. The ropes that had once bound her to Mum's madness had been cut, and she was finally free to grow in the rich soil of Canada.

At the airport, as Shell passed through the first gate of security, she paused and looked back at me. She smiled at me and mouthed, 'I love you.'

I smiled and waved back, silently mouthing, 'I love you too.' As her figure disappeared, my legs trembled beneath me. The tears came fast, and my breath caught in my throat. I found the nearest seat and buried my face in my hands, trying to quell the rush of air that now escaped my chest. I wept uncontrollably. It was the loneliest I'd ever felt.

I have never told Shell of the devastation I felt when she left that day. It was as if I was losing Dad all over again. She was only a flight away, but I was losing my sister, my soulmate and the only person who understood me and the pain we both felt. I could only selfishly think that God was disciplining me once again – but for what, I could not fathom. I knew then, deep down, that although our river would remain, our streams had diverted, never to fully merge again.

* * *

Loneliness was a constant voice in my head and, without Shell, the echo became louder and more domineering. She'd always been the strongest, the one who'd stood in command to fend off attacks whenever we felt outnumbered. She was my right arm, and without her my life felt unbalanced, constantly teetering on the edge of the cliff. Who would hold me when I was sad? Who would tell me to get a grip when I felt lost? More importantly, who was going to let me beat them at wrestling? Who was going to make to laugh with just a look and a twitch of her nose? Who would throw custard at the wall with me now?

I moved into my new home. Its small but airy rooms radiated a warmth that instantly made any anxious person feel at ease. I felt that the house had only been witness to happy sounds, and I was confident that feelings of love permeated the walls. On the days Hayley was with Darryl, I filled the lonely hours by painting walls, scrubbing skirting boards, and fixing broken furniture. Luckily for me, Canada's electrical supply was incompatible with English currents, so I'd been left most of Shell's white goods and her large, modern TV. The only things that I had to find were new beds and a coffee table. The coffee table came from Argos and needed assembling. With the help of a butter knife and sheer determination, the form of a table emerged before me. I sat on the floor, admiring my handiwork, and said, 'Who needs screwdrivers and a man? Are you proud of me, Dad?'

Of course there was no reply.

My smile evaporated. 'Are you there, Dad?'

The tears began to flow once more. 'I need you.'

12

FROM THE OUTSIDE LOOKING IN

'Why does my "bag for life" weigh so heavy?' I ask God.
'Because it is full of good things to eat,
and good things are heavy.'
'But the weight of the bag is leaving marks on
the palm of my hand and pain in my shoulder.'
'You have to bear the weight to
reap the benefits of that goodness.'
'That's all well and good, God . . . but can't you
throw in a chocolate doughnut and a can of
Stella every now and again?'

I was in the corridor at work. I stood still, lurking behind a door, and peered through at my friend as she hugged her dad. He smiled at her as only a father could, and the envy bubbled. I was looking through a window, looking in on a normal thirty-two-year-old's life. I thought for a moment about the family I wanted, the family I should have had. I took a deep breath and shook my head fiercely, wiping away the self-pity, and continued down the corridor to my next patients.

It had been nearly a year since Shell left, and I was acting as Mum's fulltime carer, just as Dad had before me, as the government refused to accept responsibility. Mum was now living in a one-bedroom flat, which was much easier for me to maintain. Of course, my work wasn't always met with thanks. On one occasion, I brought Mum to my home to do her washing and have lunch. Mum looked upon the windowsills, spotting Hayley and Dad's smiling faces captured within a single wooden frame. A sudden and dramatic change occurred.

'Why aren't there any photos of me?'

'I don't have any nice photos of you, Mum,' I explained.

She sat on the sofa in silence. I could practically see the devil whispering in her ear, wriggling and teasing, pushing aside her rational thoughts. After about a minute, she leapt from the sofa and headed towards the kitchen. As I emerged from the living room, she spun around and thrust the sharp blade of a bread knife dangerously close to my face. She breathed hard.

'Mum, put the knife down,' I said.

'You hate me, don't you?' she spat, the knife waving in front of my cheek.

'No, I don't hate you, Mum.'

'Then why?' she asked, her hand now shaking.

'I don't understand, Mum. What is it?'

She hesitated and lowered her hand. 'Just give me my washing and take me home.'

'Give me the knife and I will take you home, okay?'

As I waited for the washing cycle to finish, Mum sat on the sofa and watched me with the look of a woman who hated what she saw. The noise of the final spin cycle vibrated in the air. Finally, I loaded her laundry into the boot of the car and waited for her to climb into the passenger seat. As her hands were full of groceries, I leaned over from the driver's seat and opened the passenger door for her. As it swung open, it hit Mum in the chest, and she fell into the road like a wounded rabbit. For a second, I wondered whether I had done it on purpose. Either way, I quickly left the security of my seat and ran around to the passenger side of my car, where I lifted Mum from the road.

The five-mile drive back to Mum's flat felt like a hundred, as Mum's anger filled the small confines of the car. When we finally arrived, I carried the heavy bags of washing and groceries to the small but snug flat and quickly turned to leave. At the back gate, Mum stood, altercation written on her face and in her stance. As I moved to pass her, she hissed without words. Once again, I motioned to move past her and, as I did, her fist rose to collide with my chin. Did she mean to hurt me? Or was it a desperate act to show her grievance? Whatever it meant, it was an act that a mother should never bestow upon her child.

The following week, I returned to the small flat to clean, the confrontation already forgotten by Mum. All I could do was bury this latest abuse deep and pretend that all was forgiven.

* * *

The routine of Mum's illness continued, and I bounced around her constant and demanding moods while trying to deal with my own feelings of hopelessness. Even work could not provide the sanctuary I hoped for, for there was the constant fear that I would get the phone call that came two or three times a year. The voice of a colleague would sound out the battle cry: 'It's your mum on the phone.'

My pace would slow, my heart would quicken and my hands would start to shake.

'Hi Mum,' I said once, hoping that none of my colleagues would guess that there was a screaming woman on the other end of the line.

'Why did you say that I was a bad mother?' came Mum's venomous voice.

'What? What are you on about, Mum?'

'I am not a bad mother, you bitch.'

'But I didn't . . .'

'Well you won't have to put up with a no-good mother anymore. I've taken an overdose.' When I didn't respond, she shouted, 'I want to die!'

I hung my head low, hoping to disguise the screams emanating from the handset. The phone fell silent. I phoned an ambulance and left work. I felt no alarm, no panic – I'd learnt the hard way that Mum's suicidal pronouncements were no more than dramatic demands for attention.

As I neared the flat, I spotted flashing blue lights up ahead. I arrived to a scene of pure chaos. Two crew members were struggling to take basic observations from the screaming woman sitting defiantly on the sofa.

'Linda, how many tablets have you taken?'

'Fuck off,' was her reply. 'Let me die.'

'Mum, stop it, they are just trying to help you,' I said in the most controlled voice I could muster.

I introduced myself with an apologetic smile and opened the back door to help clear the fog of cigarette smoke that was starting to sting my eyes.

'Mum, put your fag out so they can help you.'

'What are you doing here, you bitch?'

One of the paramedics turned to look at me, and all I could do was smile in embarrassment. I looked around the sitting room, finding fag ash scattered like fairy dust over every inch of the carpet. Stray mugs were scattered around, stained deep brown from many days of neglect. Shoes and slippers lay unwanted and abandoned on the sofa alongside discarded underwear and tea-stained T-shirts. Shame gripped me, and it took all that I had to stop the tears bubbling to the surface. How could I allow Mum to live this way? I felt as if I had failed her, not only in terms of support but basic care too. How could I have let Mum reach this point? Why had I not seen this coming? I was a bad daughter, a terrible person.

Mum ended up staying overnight in A&E with a

stomach pump and a psychiatric assessment to add to her ever-growing medical records. For the next two years, I remained trapped in a world that I could not control. On bad days, I found myself hating Mum, wishing that she'd finally succeed in her feeble attempts at suicide. I followed a lonely cycle of guilt and hatred, with my mum at the centre.

* * *

It has been said that if a door is slammed in your face, go open a window. I met Jason on my computer window, and thankfully he unlocked it for me. He was like no one I had ever met before, and he brought excitement into my other-wise stress-filled life. Being from London, Jason took me to romantic restaurants and West End shows. I started to find laughter again, and maybe I started to see happiness just around the corner.

It was difficult for Jason to understand my relationship with Mum and even more difficult for me to explain it. When things were bad it was easy for him to unplug the phone and ignore her demands, but for me it was the guilt that pulled me to her door. He couldn't understand why I would have someone in my life that gave nothing but pain. On the rare occasions that Jason joined me on a visit, the conversations with Mum were strained and uneasy. She would glare at him with narrowed eyes and thin lips as the room filled with cigarette smoke. Jason would stand in the garden unable to cope with the stinging eyes and coughing.

Mum would regard this as a personal rebuff until it climaxed into a full-on attack.

'He can cut my grass, but if he tries to come inside I will stab him in the heart!' was the greeting on one such visit. Their relationship now wavers between tolerance and defence: Mum defending her ownership of me and Jason defending my sanity. At last I felt that someone had seen me on the other side of the window and was unlocking the latch.

Then God once again demanded discipline.

'It's cancer, Lisa,' Shell said in a quiet, controlled voice. The phone crackled with silence as I began to understand the words she had just spoken.

'*No, no, no, no . . .*' I cried. 'It can't be.' The anguish poured from me as great sobs that just wouldn't stop. Jason sat bolt upright and hugged me tight without saying a word. I just couldn't believe that this was happening again. How would God justify it this time? What had I done to deserve more discipline, more pain? What had Shell done to be punished in this way? An overwhelming feeling of hatred for God streamed through my brain, and I wanted to scream.

'Lisa, Lisa, it's okay, please, it's okay,' Shell struggled to say through her own tears. 'It's thyroid cancer. The doctor said it's easily treated, but I've got to have the whole thing out and then some radiation treatment.'

The phone was silent, and all that I could hear was Shell's gentle respiration. Fear started to trickle down the length of my spine.

'I am scared, Lisa.'

At last, Shell was telling me the truth. My anguish calmed as my sobs receded. 'I know, Shell, but you will beat this. I promise.'

* * *

Within a couple of weeks, I was in Canada. Shell lay immobile in the hospital bed, a catheter draining fluid from the wound in her neck. She could only whisper short bursts of words as her throat was still bruised and inflamed from the operation to remove the cancer. The ward was uncomfortably hot, and I felt stifled by the heavy jumper I was wearing. It was strangely silent despite the nurses fussing over IV lines and medical charts. Shell's eyes fluttered open and then immediately closed again, heavy with tiredness. I held her hand and kissed her gently on her damp, hot cheek.

Her eyes remained closed as she turned and smiled at me. 'Hi,' she whispered.

'Hi, sis. How are you doing?'

'Felt better,' Shell replied as she struggled to swallow. 'It's painful to swallow, let alone talk.'

'Well, stop talking then!'

Shell tried to laugh but all that left her swollen throat was a small gush of air. I turned to look at Russ, who was occupying the children at the end of the bed. 'Shell's awake,' I whispered. As Russ moved to sit by his wife, my three-year-old nephew Nathan climbed onto my lap and clung tightly to my chest. I tried to gently encourage Nathen to look at his Mum. 'Say hi to Mummy,' I said, but instead he buried his face deep into my jumper and quietly murmured.

'It's okay, Lee. Why don't you take them outside to play?'

Leaving Russ and Shell alone, I took Nathen and his younger sister, Hannah, outside to the children's play area. Away from the alien and frightening scene both children changed into balls of energy. I scooped Nathen and Hannah up into my arms and hugged them closely, when Nathen whispered in my ear, 'Are you my new mummy now?'

'No, sweetie. Mummy will be home soon.'

Three months later, I was back in Canada. It was time for the radioactive poison to do its job. Shell described it as tasting like stale vodka, but hopefully that stale vodka would kill her cancerous cells and free her from the family's growing cancer club. For the next three weeks, Shell was radioactive and was thus confined alone to a two-metre world bound by barriers. As Shell's children were too young to understand the exclusion rules, Shell was sent to stay at her in-laws' empty house on the other side of the city, to contemplate her fate alone. When she felt well, I took her out for coffee, sitting outside the instructed two-metre barrier. When I felt the coast was clear, I would sneak in a cuddle and a kiss and then quickly return to the exclusion zone, hoping that no one from the hospital would catch me breaking the rules.

* * *

Aside from the fading garrotte line across her throat, Shell has fully recovered and is happy. On occasion, we revisit the subject, mainly by making jokes about how she was a 'radioactive superwoman' or about the Halloween just after, when she dressed up as Frankenstein's monster, sporting her very own (and very real!) cut throat. But the conversation always ends in silent contemplation as the memories bubble deep, causing the sadness to open the dusty boxes in our minds. We look at each other, trying to stifle the pain that presses on our tear ducts, communicating comfort over the internet with pixilated faces and robotic *I love you*s.

13
MY LOST SHOE

It was September 12th, 2009 at around 3:45 p.m. when I could take it no more. I raised my white flag and said, 'I can't do this anymore. Enough now.' My stamina had faded, my strength had been broken and I gave up. To admit defeat was the easy part – to live with the decision was the hardest.

It was the time of year that filled me with dread. I had that feeling you get when your fight-or-flight response kicks into overdrive, filling you with terror and breaking the connection between your body and brain. For most people, this is sparked by the sight of a spider or the view from a very tall building or bridge, but for me it was Mum's annual doctor review meeting, which determined her eligibility for benefits. It started as soon as the letter arrived at her door. Then the phone calls began, arriving throughout the night; sometimes they were calm declarations of suicide, and sometimes she screamed how she hated me. Even though I constantly told myself that it was the illness talking, the words still stabbed hard at my heart and soon had me sobbing on Jason's shoulder. Although I had become accustomed to the insults and physical hurt over the years, every word and every action still cut deep.

We sat in the small, suffocating holding room, waiting to be seen by the doctor. A man with a knee brace sat opposite, on a bank of four chairs welded together at the arms, and a young woman with tired dark eyes sat to my right. Mum stood pensively in front of the water fountain, her eyes fixed on me. I could feel her anxiety and the anger that was building. A woman with short grey hair and a white tunic entered the room and asked for the woman with tired eyes to follow her. The shift of atmosphere seemed to unsettle Mum, and she stiffened. I shifted uncomfortably in my seat. The clock rang on in the silence, and with every tick I wished that time could whisk me away.

Suddenly I was soaked. Mum had thrown her polystyrene cup at my face. 'Give me back my husband!' she screamed. 'Give me back my husband.' She was just inches from my face.

I sat motionless, water running down my face, embarrassed.

'Bitch, why did you take my husband away?'

I remained silent, hoping that she might forget about me and leave me alone. How could she think I'd ever give her back my dad when in life she had tortured him so?

'I hate you,' she continued, throwing another polystyrene cup my way.

The next few minutes felt like a thousand. Finally, the lady with grey hair returned to the room and asked for Mum to follow her. Mum stared at me, her cold eyes sending a shiver through me, and left the room. I finally released the breath that I'd unknowingly been holding, and at once the tears arrived. The man with the leg brace asked if I was okay. I was too embarrassed to make eye contact, and without lifting my head, I said, 'Yes, I am fine, thanks.'

The grey-haired lady returned to the room with a box of tissues and handed them to me without a word. All I wanted her to say was, 'Are you okay?' or 'Can I help?' but she said nothing.

I sat there alone, frantically trying to think of what I had done to deserve the bitterness that Mum had thrown my way and what I could do to diffuse the conflict that was about to be thrust upon me. I could only hope that when the assessment was over, Mum would be calm. My hopes were shattered when I heard a familiar scream. Mum was shrieking some unintelligible conversation, and the hairs stood proud on the back of my neck. I buried my head in my hands, hoping that the screaming would stop, but it went on. I remained motionless for what felt like days, but the screaming still did not subside.

I couldn't ignore it any longer; if I didn't act now I knew it wouldn't end well. I stood and moved towards the sound of Mum's screams, her cries acting as my beacon. As I neared, the monster emerged from a door to my right, quickly followed by a pale man with terror in his eyes. Mum pushed me aside without acknowledging my presence, and the distressed man turned to me. 'Well, I can see that she really is ill.'

I looked at the doctor, my eyes full of tears, and without saying a word I pleaded with him to help me. His face ghostly white, he stared at me, and for a moment I was unsure whether he'd understood my secret message. He looked suddenly at the ground and cleared his throat, and I felt the agonising, inconvenient conflict that I had caused him. He turned without speaking, walked into his office and closed the door behind him. I was left in the dim corridor alone.

Mum was waiting outside the drab, official-looking building, a cigarette tightly pursed between her lips. It was a warm day for September, but I felt the icy bite in the air surrounding the woman who waited for me. She said nothing, but her look told me that the end of the assessment had done nothing to quell the hatred burning inside her.

'Stay there, Mum. I will go get the car,' I said, hoping for a few minutes of peace before the impending altercation. Again, she said nothing, but she lit a second cigarette while crushing the butt of the previous one under her foot.

I sat for a while in the car, looking at my swollen red face in the rear-view mirror. All I wanted was to drive home, but the thought of Mum wandering the streets alone filled me with guilt, and the weight of my responsibility persuaded me to put the car into gear and return to the woman I was beginning to hate.

Mum remained in the spot where I had left her, a pile of cigarette butts at her feet. She watched me bring the car to a stop at the curb. I took a sharp breath in, hoping that the few minutes we spent apart had been long enough to quench her anger. As soon as she opened the car door, I knew that I was wrong. She tossed a folded piece of paper at my face. 'Slut,' she said as the paper fell into my lap. 'The man in the waiting room gave me his number for you. You should go home and shag your boyfriend instead, you slut.'

Mum turned to face me and then spat in my face.

I was silent for a moment. Slowly, I turned to look through the windscreen and tried to focus on the lives unfolding outside. An old lady in a long red raincoat pulled a tartan shopping trolley, and I imagined a packet of custard creams sitting atop tins of baked beans and vegetable soup. A young woman pushed a buggy, the child within crying and reaching for a lost shoe on the pavement. The mother bent to retrieve the lost shoe and handed it back to her child before kissing the top of her baby's head. The child stopped crying and waved the shoe in the air and giggled.

It began to rain. The droplets of water ran like over-flowing streams finding new paths around the imperfections in the glass, and I imagined the explosion of the water's origin. I couldn't hear Mum's continuing abuse, only comprehending a background murmur that interrupted my thoughts. Outside, the world went by, and I waited for the strength I needed to fend off the escalating attack, but it never came. What little self-respect I had lay lifeless like the spit gathered on my shirt.

I put the car into first gear and pulled out of the car park.

For forty minutes, I drove without really seeing the road. All I saw were trees and lampposts, and I wondered what it would feel like to aim the bonnet of the car towards them. Would it be painful? More painful than living? Mum continued to scream, and she told me how all her agonies were my fault. The murkiness of my tears muddied the road, and I drove from memory, following only blurred white lines.

'I hate you,' she repeated over and over again. 'You have killed me.' Without warning, she began to slam her head against the passenger window in a rhythm that matched every scream. 'Just kill me now, kill me,' she screamed again. Over and over, she pounded the side of her head against the glass, and I feared the window would shatter at any moment.

Without a second thought, I stopped the car suddenly. 'Get out!' I screamed.

'I hate you,' she repeated, but this time she leaned in so close that I felt the heat of her words on my face.

'I hate you too. Get out!'

Mum slammed the car door behind her and kicked it, almost pushing her off balance. I left without looking back. I didn't care that I was leaving her behind, I didn't care that she was alone, I didn't care that she was my mum. I couldn't indulge the sight of her walking away and risk guilt guiding me back.

It was that day that I gave up. I just didn't possess the strength. I was weak, and I had failed Mum. I had renounced my position as punchbag, carer and daughter, and I felt no guilt. It had become clear to me that I simply couldn't help Mum anymore. I was unable to save her from the ocean, unable to pull her up from the jagged rocks that trapped her. The silent sea creatures swam unnoticed between her fingers, and the air drained from her lungs. My mum had drowned. I had lost my grip on her hand, and as I struggled to find air to breathe, I lost her. It would be six months before we would talk again, and another six before I could face swimming out again into the darkness.

14

A GAME OF RANDOM SELECTION

Time is a liability when you have to wait. The tick of every second sounds louder than the second before, and moments seem to elongate as they pass. The seconds tease you with the promise of fulfilment and potential, so why do we so often waste those seconds? We kill time when we cannot fill it, so why in the end do we wish for more? More time in the day, more time on holiday, more time to live.

I was dealt the thirteenth tarot card – Death — eighteen months after Shell, at the age of forty. It wasn't the end, but the beginning of the next chapter in my life of struggle. In a game of chance, God got His finger caught in the spinning roulette wheel, and it fell on my number. Sometimes I feel it wasn't an accident at all, but a purposeful hand that stopped the wheel and a defiant finger that pointed at me.

The tumour that was growing in my right breast was just 'one of those things', something that happened for no reason with no justification. 'We just don't know why,' the consultant told me. I peered into the kind face of the surgeon who'd broken the bad news, but I didn't hear what he was saying. His face began to merge with the face of the quiet doctor who'd told me that Dad was going to die, and his voice began to sound like Shell had when she'd told me how scared she was. The words *surgery*, *chemotherapy* and *radiotherapy* bounced around the room, but all I could manage to do was nod every now and again, pretending to understand. Jason held my hand tightly. If it weren't for him asking questions and paying attention, I would have left the room, thinking that this strange man had just spent ten minutes telling me a story about some other woman who had breast cancer.

As I left the consultation room, Jason hugged me and asked if I was okay. 'No,' I said. 'I just want to go home.'

* * *

I sat on the bedroom floor, pulling the long fibres out of the carpet. I looked at the lengths of silvery synthetic wool, and as I gently blew, they floated away on the small gust, only to land a few inches upon the very carpet I'd plucked them from. Jason sat next to me, and we were silent. The room was spinning, and I began to feel sick. Tears crept into my mouth, and the salty taste added to the nausea that rose inside me. I turned to look at Jason. His tears were heavy, but I felt the strength emanating from his firm grip upon my hand, and I smiled. The silence between us said a thousand words, and we remained on the carpet until the sky darkened outside the window and tiredness drove us to sleep.

* * *

Hayley had just turned sixteen, and it was graduation day. It was the day after my first dose of chemotherapy, and not even the nausea and vengeful reflux were going to stop me taking my rightful place as Hayley's mother, watching her transform into a beautiful young lady. I stood in the unseasonal hot weather and fought to remain standing, my legs like jelly. The pain echoed through my bones, and I wished for every second to speed by so I could collapse into a chair. As the line of Ferraris and open-topped cars passed, I felt the poison flowing through my veins, gradually draining my low reserves of energy. I was about to ask Jason to help me back to the car when Hayley's small black wedding car appeared in sight. The sight of Hayley sent energy surging through my fading muscles, and I mustered the will to smile and wave. Pride swept through me as I watched her step from the car and enter the next chapter of her life. As soon as she was out of sight, I fell back into Jason. 'Let's go,' I said.

* * *

That night, I lay with my head on Jason's chest. I tried to lift my head from the gentle undulations of his breathing, but found I could not. After a moment of straining, I cried, 'I just can't do this, Jason. Is this what it's supposed to feel like?'

'I don't know,' Jason replied, helplessness in his voice. I knew that he could not tell me that everything would be okay; he couldn't guarantee that. All he could do was hold me and ignore the pool of tears that was now gathering in his belly button.

Over the next few days, the pain ceased, and I got used to the overwhelming fatigue, which transformed me into an arthritic eighty-year-old. To cheer me up, Jason booked a few days in a cottage in Wales so that we could hide from the cancer that had invaded our home. I had strict instructions from the oncology unit to be wary of infection, as chemotherapy could kill good cells as well as the bad, and having an infection blurred that distinction. In the packed bag of knickers and beer, a supply of infection-fighting gels and wipes mingled with a thermometer and the anti-sickness drugs that I always kept close.

After a day in Portmeirion, following in the footsteps of Patrick McGoohan running from big, bouncing white balloons, we settled by the open fire with cheese and red wine. It was June, but it was still Wales, and I just could not get warm. Even after soaking in a steaming-hot bath and wrapping myself in blankets, I shivered in front of the fire. I couldn't admit to Jason just how ill I felt. The little energy that I retained had left me, and it hurt to let the cold Welsh air into my lungs. The thermometer showed that my temperature was normal, meaning there was no infection to worry about, so I couldn't understand why I felt so bad. I struggled on, pretending that all was well, until a suggested walk from Jason was the final straw.

'You don't understand!' I screamed.

He sat quietly, hurt by my outburst.

With words muffled by tears I said, 'I just can't do it, Jason. I can't carry on pretending that everything is normal.'

'Do you think I don't care or understand?' Jason replied with a mixture of hurt and anger in his voice. I began to cry full tears and hid my face in the blanket wrapped around my shoulders. No one spoke; we only sat motionless on the small sofa.

My initial frustration began to calm, and I whispered, 'I am sorry. I didn't mean to shout at you. I don't really expect you to understand, and I know you do care.' I paused, waiting for Jason to tell me it was okay. It came in the form of a hug, and I melted into his body and began to feel okay.

As every muscle in my body started to burn, I finally admitted that I couldn't carry on. My façade had failed, and I turned to Jason for help. We returned home, and as I climbed into yet another steaming-hot bath, I combed my fingers through my hair, only to see my hand covered in long, dark strands. I had failed to notice the small pile of hair that lay on the bathroom floor, and although I'd known this day would come, the horror took my breath away. On top of my odd-looking, post-lumpectomy breast, the loss of my hair was a sign of cancer that would be hard to deny. It was the sign that the cancer would change everything, including the person I used to be, and once again I found that I had lost complete control over my body. Cancer was now my new enemy, my new battle – but unlike anorexia, I could not stop it from taking me alone. I'd need faith on my side.

* * *

The clippers buzzed behind me, and I heard Jason ask if I was sure that this is what I wanted to do.

'Yes,' I replied, certainty in my voice.

'I can't do it,' he said at last through rapid bursts of tears. 'I can't believe this is happening. I can't do it.'

My own tears began to fall, but I held fast. 'There's no point in holding on to it; I am going to be bald in a week or so anyway. Besides, if I turn into Kojak, I can at least have lots of lollipops,' I joked.

Jason didn't laugh.

When it was done, I lay in the steaming bath, running my hand over the hard, spiky bristles of my scalp. I felt cold. There were dark speckles of hair stuck to my hand, and I quickly tried to brush them off. Of course, the dampness of my hand only attracted more, and I felt an odd panic as they clung to me. I frantically washed them away underneath the water as if they were toxic chemicals. The hairs rose to the soapy surface of the bathwater and clung to my thighs. I scrambled up, but the heat of the water and my spent energy made the escape slow and clumsy. Jason entered the bathroom, finding me motionless and breathless on the edge of the bath, staring down at my pale and blotchy skin.

'Come on, you,' he said. 'It can't be that bad.'

I managed a smile and lifted myself from my seat. 'Perhaps I just need feeding,' I lied.

* * *

Wrapped in jumpers and dressing gowns, I lifted the banana to my mouth, knowing that I needed to eat. I opened my mouth, but my jaw felt tight, as though the bones had been fused together. I tried again but failed once more.

* * *

Neutropenia is a type of infection that fights neutrophils, white blood cells that protect the human body from invading bacteria. Adults with any fewer than 1,500 neutrophils are considered to suffer from neutropenia; I had zero.

The oncology nurse hurried from the small room at the rear of the unit, worry etched on her face. 'Okay,' she said, hovering above my chair. 'This is the situation, Lisa.'

I was confined, alone, to a side room. The risk of infection was too high for the open ward and the company of people, so I was exiled to lonely distress and fear. I spent four days attached to a life-giving antibiotic drip that remained in constant action, night and day, and was set loose only to shower. I would linger longer than expected in the small, sterile shower room so that I could feel party to the world outside, even if only for a few minutes. I'd peer through the large sash window that sat above the white plastic seat at the busy road below, watching cars vie for position on the nearby round-about. People would hurry along the pavement, unaware of the woman spying on their lives, of the envy in her eyes.

I felt as if I was hanging on the edge of the world, waiting for my invitation to rejoin the human race.

* * *

By the time I returned home, my hair had completely aban-doned me, and I'd grown used to the chill of the air on my scalp. I didn't recognise the pale face and dark eyes that peered back at me in the mirror – where had this woman come from? What had life done to her to make her look so sad and apprehensive? I felt sad for her – I wished that I could hold her and whisper healing words, but I couldn't think of any. Besides, her defeated white face seemed too far out of reach.

My body struggled not only under the three weekly infusions of toxins, but also under the series of injections necessary to increase my immunity and white blood cell count. With each impending injection into my bruised abdomen, I would sob and plead with Jason not to go through with it, as I knew that pain would follow. It would render me immobile and miserable, and in those moments, it seemed preferable to risk further episodes of neutropenia than to suffer the small needle. Nausea was my constant companion, and even the multitude of antiemetics couldn't quite keep it at bay.

For the week that preceded those immune-boosting injections, I would feel almost normal (discounting, of course, my hairless scalp). I savoured every pain-free moment by engaging in as many normal, everyday activities as possible – cleaning the oven, hanging clothes on the washing line, tidying the house.

There had been a few tentative conversations with Mum, all of them punctuated by silent pauses and stumbled words, and I felt myself pulling back from every soft word Mum uttered. I couldn't let go of the hurt she'd caused me, and although Mum asked for us to start again, my reluctance was overwhelming. I had spent my life constantly forgiving Mum for her verbal and physical abuse, and the thought of entering back into a relationship with her felt insane. No intelligent human would purposefully put themselves in harm's way – well, not unless they wanted to. Some people would call such a willingness altruism or benevolence. I wasn't prepared to endure more suffering for a moment of love that would never come.

Although Mum was aware of my illness, she barely acknowledged it. She would ask the cashier at the store to help me pack the groceries but would think nothing of asking me to Hoover her carpet or move furniture. She was consumed by her own self-pity, her demons preventing the outside world from permeating the bubble that encased her. I was not expecting the support that would be normal for a mother to give, but it did not stop me from longing for it. The mental divide between us had started to soften, and I could sense a change in Mum that resonated unease. I could not bring myself to lower my guard; I had been fooled too many times before. Still, I couldn't help wondering whether Mum had at last learnt to ignore the devil that spoke to her. Had an epiphany struck, allowing her to acknowledge me as her daughter? Had the six months without me made her realise that she needed me as a carer and verbal punchbag? Or had the threat of death made us both reconsider the abusive relationship that danced between us? Whatever the reasons may have been, my mother and I seemed to be taking the first tentative steps towards a relationship that hinted and teased at faint echoes of love.

* * *

After six months, I returned to work, but it would take another year to complete my treatment and another year for my strength to fully return. My hair reappeared in thick, greying curls, and the scars that peppered my breast and armpit began to fade. However, even years on, I still panic at the feel of a lump or the lingering of a cough. Although the memories may fade, dust gathering on the lid of that particular box, you can without warning be reminded that cancer, like life, will never truly give you peace.

15

DREAM NOT OF YESTERDAY

Life is like shrink-wrap around a new CD. You go round and around, trying to find the little flap that will let you peel the cover off, but you can't for the life of you find it. You eventually lose patience and, in a temper, throw it down on the kitchen worktop. You stop and stare at it, wondering about the music you're missing. So after a while, when your nerves are calm, you finally find that cellophane flap and, for the next few hours, dance madly and happily around the kitchen to the magical beats once denied to you.

The cigarette smoke stung my eyes. I coughed, rousing Mum from her vacant staring, and she told me to open a window. After, I returned to my seat and glanced at Mum, who was peering into a world that was invisible to me. She was in her red armchair, surrounded by cigarette ash. Beau, her two-year-old Westiepoo, sat at her feet, which were nestled in worn, ash-covered slippers. It was two o'clock in the afternoon, but she was still wearing her dressing gown pocked with burn holes. Her sadness was evident and striking, and for a moment I wondered what she saw. Tears pressed hard at the corners of my eyes, and I felt genuine sorrow, for it must be so lonely in that world. She remained silent as I studied her eyes; she appeared to have forgotten my presence. Suddenly, she turned to me and told me that she was raped by two men at a party when she was sixteen. For what felt like an eternity, I stopped breathing. Was that what she saw in the invisible world before her? For the first time, I'd been granted a glimpse of the demons that had been taunting Mum throughout her life.

Even now, I'm not sure what brought on her sudden statement. I remained motionless, waiting for her to elaborate, tears streaking my face.

'It doesn't really matter,' she continued flatly.

The ashtray that was balanced on the arm of her chair suddenly fell, adding to the ash moat around the base of her chair. The commotion appeared to shake Mum from her memories, and I stood to clear the mess.

'Don't worry about it,' she said. 'I will clear it up later.' But she didn't protest when I cleared it up anyway, for I knew that despite her intentions, the mess would still be waiting for me on my next visit. After the whoosh of the Hoover ended and a fresh cup of tea was placed in Mum's hand, Beau settled on my lap, eyeing me expectantly.

'Did you ever tell anyone, Mum?' I said at last. Mum

laughed, causing the tea to slop over the edge of her mug. She ignored the burn of the hot water. 'No one would have believed me anyway. My mother and father were not people you could talk to.' She shifted uneasily in her chair, took another long drag of her fag, and sighed deeply. 'They were the type of people who would knock you unconscious and then leave you bleeding on the kitchen floor.' Mum paused as she rubbed the palm of her hand over her eyes before continuing. 'They weren't nice people and their arguing would never stop. I spent most of the time hiding in the garden.' Mum allowed a huff of laughter to escape but didn't tell me the joke. Her face became sombre again and she returned to the smouldering fag in her hand. 'I think I was about eleven when I broke my leg. That was Nanny's fault.'

I was confused; either her memories had fused together in one big melting pot, or she was tripping over the rush of stories, her tongue failing to keep pace with her thoughts. She stubbed her cigarette out in the empty ashtray and reached for another before taking a long, satisfying drag. Beau shuffled on my lap, and I silently recoiled as her nails dug into the exposed skin of my knees. She looked at me with disappointment in her eyes when I pulled my stroking hand away and pawed at me until I began again.

Mum was silent again, her eyes focused on the far wall. 'They weren't very nice people,' she repeated. 'My father made everyone's life miserable.'

I waited for her to continue, the unspoken question hanging in the air like a ghost. I felt like a peeping Tom, spying on Mum's private memories, and the story was confusing and nonsensical – I wondered if she was really making a confession or whether she was just reciting the story to herself out loud. 'Did you know that Nanny ended up in the same psychiatric hospital as me? He drove her to it,' she said.

'Did Nanny have mental health problems too?' I asked.

'Did she half! Right fruit loop she was,' Mum answered with a snort.

We didn't often visit Mum's parents, but I'd had no idea that Nan had suffered as much as Mum had. 'I didn't know,' I said quietly.

'No one did, really. They hid it very well.'

'How did they hide it? What happened?'

She didn't answer, but she sat silently, staring into space. I watched as her mind wandered into the invisible world again and chastised myself for pushing the inquest too far. She had been reciting her memories as if they were of a trip to the supermarket or the horror film she'd watched, and I wondered just how deep those memories had been buried. Maybe she'd finally given up on the idea that burying her trauma would render it idle and harmless. Maybe she truly didn't know the answers to my questions.

'Ooh, did you see the last episode of *Dexter* last night? I do like him, he's a good baddie,' Mum said suddenly, knowing full well that I had never seen an episode.

'No, Mum, I didn't see it,' I said.

'It was a good one last night; I really thought they were going to catch him. Do you want a cup of tea, love?'

I looked down at my full mug of cold tea. 'I'll put the kettle on,' I said, sensing that the concrete lid of her memory was now closed.

As I returned with two mugs of hot tea, I sensed a change. Mum remained in the same dusty red chair, yet another cigarette hanging from the corner of her mouth, but Beau was no longer in the room. The patio door was open wide, and a cold draft moved through the long blue curtains, revealing the overgrown garden of nettles behind. I placed the mug of tea on the small table in front of Mum and pulled my thin cardigan tight around my chest. 'Why is the door open?' I asked as Beau entered from the bedroom.

'Why won't you let me go on holiday?' Mum retorted.

'Sorry?' I replied.

'You said I wasn't allowed to go on holiday.' The anger in her voice tells me that I should tread carefully, my shield ready.

'Don't be daft,' I said cheerfully. 'Why would I say that?'

'I don't know; perhaps you don't want me to be happy. Perhaps you don't want me to spend my money.'

My mouth was dry. 'Of course I want you to be happy, Mum, don't be silly.'

The attempt to lighten the mood failed. Mum sat bolt upright and turned on me, eyes blazing. 'I am not stupid. I know exactly what you are doing. You want me to die so you can have all my money. You are evil!' The cigarette between her stained yellow fingers trembled in her hand.

'I am going to go now, Mum, because I don't want to say something I'll regret.' I stood and bent to retrieve my bag.

'Go on then, leave, but you are not having any of my money! Get out!'

Even after all those years and the thousand cycles of abuse, it still hurt. I sobbed all the way home.

Mum stared hard at the piece of paper held in front of her. 'House, pen, hat, and pony,' she said.

'Okay, now what is today's date?' the psychiatrist asked, taking the sheet of paper away, folding it neatly and placing it on top of her desk.

'Twenty-seventh of January,' Mum replied.

Mum and I sat on uncomfortable metal chairs in the psychiatrist's office. Mum was hunched over, her hands between her knees, like a child being tested on her times tables. She peered intently and suspiciously at the petite woman opposite her.

'Now,' the psychiatrist said, 'tell me what was written on this sheet of paper.' She pointed to the folded paper on her desk.

Mum recited the words perfectly without pausing.

Why is she doing a dementia test? I wondered.

The psychiatrist turned and wrote some notes in a brown folder that lay open on her desk. Mum's intense gaze never left the woman's face, and I felt a familiar helplessness gather.

The psychiatrist turned back to Mum and took a deep breath. 'Your GP wrote to me asking for a review of your medication, is that right?'

'Yes,' Mum replied, eyes narrowed.

'Your GP has explained to you that you cannot continue to take twenty-four lorazepam a day. The recommended dose is just two per day.'

'Mum calls them Ativan,' I said, but the petite woman ignored me.

'I can't cope without them,' Mum said, desperation building in her voice. 'I don't care if they give me a heart attack; I'd be dead without them anyway.' She rocked back against the chair and sighed loudly.

'We are going to give you something to help with the side effects from coming off the lorazepam . . . I mean, the Ativan,' the psychiatrist said, turning to another woman in the room. 'Quetiapine is an anti-psychotic and should help to reduce the withdrawal symptoms and the paranoia.'

I felt Mum's intense gaze harden. The psychiatrist told her how she'd write to her GP and that her new prescription would be available next week.

The women stood, indicating that the conversation was over, and my rising dismay left my body as a gust of tumbling words. 'Is that it?'

'Are you okay?' the second woman asked.

'Not really,' I replied. 'Why can't this process be done in a controlled environment, like in the unit? I really don't think we can do this alone.' I sounded desperate, and my voice began to tremble.

'This unit is for addictions that need close observations. The withdrawal from alcohol, for example, can lead to vomiting and, in some cases, death. The withdrawal from lorazepam will not kill your mum.' For the first time, the psychiatrist acknowledged my presence.

'The withdrawal might not kill her, but suicide will,' I replied as I stood to leave the room.

As the woman prepared to respond, Mum stood and pushed herself into the psychiatrist, standing so close that their noses almost touched. 'If you don't give me my fucking pills,' she said, 'I'll smash your fucking face in.'

The psychiatrist opened the door and asked us to leave, her face void of any emotion.

I pulled Mum from the intense standoff and, in the car, collapsed into the driver's seat. I looked at Mum, who was lighting yet another cigarette, and I allowed the feelings of failure to sweep through me. I had once again failed to make the medical professionals understand the desperation that both Mum and I felt. We were desperate in different ways, but both ended the same way: with hopelessness.

'I am sorry, Mum,' I said without lifting my gaze from my twisted hands.

'They're all liars anyway,' she responded without emotion, and she threw her fag from the car window.

'Looks like we're on our own.'

Mum turned to look at me with a clarity in her eyes I had never seen before. The compassion and sorrow I felt at that moment was overwhelming, and I leaned over to hug her. For the first time, I cried not for what Mum had done, but for what had been done to her.

* * *

Over the following few months, I became once again accustomed to the demonic calls of a desperate woman and the regurgitation of medical histories to countless emergency department staff members. The ten-percent reduction of lorazepam worked until Mum got to day five and found the blister pack was empty; without the additional twenty-four pills on day six, she'd descend into a state of panic and psychosis. The once-suppressed noradrenalin would be released in a surge, frying Mum's mind and plunging her into anxiety, depression and paranoia and the guaranteed blame that would fall on her daughters.

Although the psychiatrist had stressed that Mum's withdrawal would not be physical, she complained constantly of diarrhoea, breathing difficulties and muscle pain – but for both Mum and me, it was the emotional withdrawal that was crippling. There was nothing that I could say or do to calm her frenzied and furious thoughts, and Mum would find herself whipped up into whirlwinds of conflict and mania that no one seemed to know how to placate. The absence of support was deafening, and the loneliness I felt almost crushed me. I felt I should be banging on doors and demanding help, but so many were locked from the inside.

* * *

Mum sat, once again, in her red chair, surrounded by a barricade of ash, a fag hanging limply from the corner of her mouth. Her legs were crossed, revealing the red blotches of itchy flesh that had developed since the withdrawal program started six months ago. The lack of sun had rendered her skin pale and gaunt, as the pain in her joints allowed for little time spent outside. It was day two of the weekly cycle, so Mum was calm. I was busy pulling weeds in the overgrown garden, Beau weaving between my legs and pawing at my feet. Mum's red chair was turned to the open patio doors so that she could watch my progress, and she was reciting the details of her turbulent night of sleeplessness and diarrhoea. I continued pulling nettles and grass, occasionally acknowledging her words with an encouraging nod of agreement. The sun was bright, and I was grateful for the heat. I stood from the bald patch of earth and wiped the sweat from my brow. I caught Mum smiling at me.

'Thanks, Lee,' she said. 'I don't know what I would do without you.' She finished with a sip of cold tea.

'You're welcome, Mum,' I replied, holding back the lump growing in my throat.

Suddenly, without warning or emotion, she said, 'I love you,' for what felt like the very first time.

I turned away from her, allowing the tears to fall. 'I love you too,' I whispered.

16

SOME KIND OF HAPPINESS

Some would say that I am fated to follow the predetermined path of the women in my family. Perhaps they're right – perhaps, if I do nothing to stop the process, fate will guide me on the path to depression, paranoia and delusion. Maybe even if I try to change course, fate will force me back and I will suffer anyway. Should I just sit back and submit to the fact that I can't change the genes I was born with? Is my destiny determined entirely by my past? Or, by recognising the patterns of cause and effect that have moulded my life, can I change fate? Have Shell and I bucked the trend and re-rooted the genetic tree? Yes: we determined that our lives would not follow the templates drawn up for us by fate, genetics or the past. We knew we could not allow depression to rule our lives.

When the dark times enter our minds and depression seems to be controlling our actions and thoughts, Shell and I draw on the memories that caused us to walk this road in the first place. We remember the pain and suffering that depression caused, and the overwhelming loss. This illness stole our lives, and trying to bury it deep or deny it would only destroy us and the life of the woman that it controlled. As soon as I feel the grip of anxiety and darkness trying to weed its way through my defences, I stop and remember. I will not let it control me; I will not let it steal my life; I will not let the cycle continue. Our families must not suffer as Shell, Dad and I have.

Today I am driving the six miles from my house to see Mum. A flutter of anxiety beats at the walls of my heart, and I wonder which version of Mum I will be visiting today. She phoned me this morning to tell me that the man on TV said that the government is stopping all benefits, so she might as well leave home now before she is evicted. After desperately trying to convince her that she doesn't need to gather her belongings in a red polka-dot hanky and hang them from a stick, I decided it was best to face her head-on.

As I open her front door, I am met by Beau, who frantically wedges her snout through the narrow gap, trying to escape the confines of the bungalow. Mum is, as always, on her red chair in the sitting room, smoking. In front of her stands a suitcase with what appears to be a blue pair of knickers peeking from the partially closed lid. I smile to myself, inwardly rolling my eyes.

'Ooh love, I am so glad you're here,' Mum says as I sit on the sofa opposite. 'I've been so worried.'

'You don't need to worry, Mum. Nobody is going to evict you.'

'How do you know? They did it to the man over the road.'

'No, they didn't evict him, Mum. He died!'

'That's what they want you to believe,' she says under her breath, trying to outsmart the listening devices hidden behind her sofa.

'Well, you don't have to worry about that. You will never be homeless.'

Mum sighs loudly and takes another drag from the stub of cigarette smouldering between her fingers.

'Where are you going to go, anyway?' I ask, intrigued by her runaway plan.

'Have you got a sleeping bag I could have?'

'Why do you need a sleeping bag, Mum?'

'I thought I would sleep down by the river. It would be nice and peaceful.' Before I can reply, she turns towards me. 'I got a letter today from the government telling me that they are going to stop my money. What am I going to do? I might as well die now.' She points to a white envelope on the TV stand.

I ignore her and remove the letter from its tea-stained cover and begin to read the notification from the pensions agency. As Mum has just turned seventy, it is a pension review stating that nothing will change.

After a lengthy conversation in which I finally succeed in convincing Mum to unpack her suitcase, she stands to wheel her case back to the bedroom, then turns to me and says, 'That's good, then. Let's have a cup of tea.'

* * *

So have I found happiness? Well – that's a difficult one. But I have found peace. The happiness I thought I would never feel comes in waves, cresting on ever-lingering surf. On occasion, the crests of the waves crash, only to rise again on a fresh lift of ever-moving water. Never be fooled into thinking that happiness will find you – it will not come delivered in a ribbon-tied box to your front door – you have to find it, fight for it, decide that you're deserving of it. Don't get me wrong – my bed is not made of roses yet. Panic still rushes through me when Mum's phone number flashes on my mobile, and anxiety still rages when my courage fails, but aiming to survive one second at a time is a good place to begin.

Happiness, for me, came from my determination to make it, to make my peace with life and all that God or nature had handed me. It has resulted in the past ten years of amazing memories. Without even a second thought, I have run half marathons, gone bungee jumping off of cliffs and spent a year driving around Africa in an old Land Rover Defender – and that's naming only a few of the good times. With the help of my wonderful daughter, husband, sister and friends, I finally found some kind of happiness.

It's not yet the end.

APPENDIX

Letters Home

Dear Mum,

I am writing this letter knowing that you will never read it. If you read this letter or even this book, the sleeping monster will awaken and the devil will start whispering. Talking to you about the past is very difficult and usually results only in tears and harsh words, with no good ending. I need to tell you that I forgive you. Forgiveness is a precious thing to give, and that is why it has taken me so long to give it. I forgive you, Mum, but I can't forget. Every day, I wish that things could have been different for us all, but it just wasn't to be. It took forty-seven years for me to appreciate and to understand that it was the illness that controlled you, that you were not strong enough to control it. For all that has happened, Shell and I have survived. We may have scars, but we have grown into women who have found positivity. Although we have dark sides ourselves, we have found the strength to be as normal as the next person and have our own normal, everyday family troubles. We have grown through sheer determination and have broken the cycle, and for that I am thankful. I know that I haven't told you often enough, but I love you (although it still feels uncomfortable to say those words out loud). I love you, Mum.

Lisa x

* * *

Dear Shell,

My light, my rock, my sister. The things I have learnt from you:

1. *How to win a fight by tweaking your nipples*
2. *How to moony*
3. *How to twitch my nose like a rabbit*
4. *How to make the most amazing lasagne*
5. *How to have Compassion*

The most compassionate person I have ever met is the girl who would rush out into the middle of the road to pick up an old lady who had fallen over, the girl who would give her last penny so that someone else could benefit and the girl who could comfort me with just one look. Without you, Shell, I would not have made it through those early years. The nights we spent hiding under blankets and in cupboards with our eyes closed and hands over our ears are times that I will remember with a special significance that only you and I will ever feel. I know that sometimes happiness feels a million miles away and the heavy hand of depression rests on our shoulders, but please remember I am always here. I wanted to say thank you, Shell. I love you more than you can ever know.

 Lisa x

* * *

Dear Dad,

 So I'm writing another letter that the recipient will never get to read, but I am hoping that you are sitting behind me now in your scruffy jeans and with your home haircut laughing at my attempts at humour. You were always so funny, finding laughter in even the most silent moments. Even when we lifted our ham sandwiches from our school lunchboxes only for firecrackers to explode, we would still laugh (even after the twentieth explosion!)

 I don't remember ever saying thank you. Without your love and support, both Shell and I would have followed the path that had been laid for us. You sacrificed so much for us, and I didn't appreciate how much you lost by keeping us safe. It couldn't have been easy to stay, and the temptation to leave the pain behind you must have been great. I don't know if I could have been as strong as you. Thank you, Dad, for you sacrifice, and I am sorry I never told you, but you can rest knowing that Shell and I are okay and living our own lives, not Mum's. I love you, Dad, and I miss you with every inch of my heart.

 Lisa x

Mum and Dad on their wedding day in 1968

Mum Shell and I 18 months old

Dad Shell and I 1972

Shell and I aged 8 years

Mum Shell and I at around 1978

Mum Christmas 1980

Dad just before he died August 2002

Shell and I June 2018 (I am the one on the left)

THANK YOU

If you enjoyed reading *Madness and Me*, please leave a review at the store you purchased it from.

Reviews are the best way to show your support for an author and to help new readers discover their books.

Made in the USA
Las Vegas, NV
24 January 2021

16460100R00105